Accession no.
36033956

WITHDRAWN

D1331517

LIS LIBRARY

Date	Fund
11 12 13.	r-che

Order No

02429287

University of Chester

WITNESS TO THE WORD

A Commentary on John 1
by
KARL BARTH

*Lectures at Münster in 1925
and at Bonn in 1933*

*Edited by Walther Fürst
and
Translated by Geoffrey W. Bromiley*

Wipf and Stock Publishers
EUGENE, OREGON

Wipf and Stock Publishers
199 West 8th Avenue, Suite 3
Eugene, Oregon 97401

Witness to the Word
A Commentary on John 1
By Barth, Karl
Copyright© January, 1986 Theologischer Verlag Zürich
ISBN: 1-59244-250-1
Publication date: June, 2003 .
Previously published by Wm. B. Eerdmans Publishing Co., January, 1986 .

Translation of pp. VII–188 of the original German edition: Karl Barth, *Erklärung des Johannes-Evangeliums (Kap. 1–8)* © 1976 by Theologischer Verlag Zürich.

CONTENTS

TRANSLATOR'S PREFACE

Barth's Lectures on John (chs. 1 – 8), which he himself did not publish, came at the important period when he was turning his attention more fully to dogmatics. Their significance will be immediately apparent to students of Barth, for, although he displayed a keen linguistic and even textual interest, theological interpretation formed his primary concern in keeping with his deepest hermeneutical convictions. In this regard he found only the slightest use for the Mandean materials that he borrowed from Bultmann, for he believed that the author, like himself, bent to his own purposes the things that he took from other sources. Of more interest to Barth was the relation that he discerned in the Gospel between revelation and the witness to revelation, for this helped to shape his own formulation of the role of the written (and spoken) Word vis-à-vis the incarnate Word. The exposition of ch. 1, to which the present translation is restricted, and which covers almost half the book, lies at the heart and basis of his own equation of revelation and incarnation, which gives to Christ, Revealer and Revealed, a crucial position in God's revealing and reconciling work, and which involves the paradox of the incognito whereby revealing is concealing except for those who by the Spirit and in faith behold the glory of the Logos. For Barth, of course, the prologue seemed so self-evidently to vindicate christological orthodoxy that he could ground his own christology in the Nicene statement and find illumination in patristic exposition. Incidentally, his discussion of the meaning of the Word's taking "flesh" exposes the emptiness of the objection sometimes raised against the *Dogmatics* that Barth impugns the sinless perfection of the Son.

Inevitably the gap between the delivery of these Lectures and their publication means that they cannot profit by the able scholarship that has been devoted to John in the intervening period. Yet they add so much to our understanding of the younger Barth and his development, and they offer such valuable insights to students of this seminal Gospel, that little excuse is needed for their belated appearance. With slight modifications (including references to English translations where available, transliterating the Greek, and some rearrangement of the paragraphs), the present translation adopts the apparatus described and used in the Swiss edition, and it takes over the Swiss indexes insofar as they relate to the first chapter of John.

Pasadena, Ascensiontide 1984   Geoffrey W. Bromiley

PREFACE

I

In Göttingen Karl Barth gave secondary lectures on various New Testament books and passages (Ephesians, James, 1 Corinthians 15, 1 John, Philippians, Colossians, and the Sermon on the Mount).[1] When he began to teach at Münster in 1925 and 1926, he offered John's Gospel as a main course, rejoicing in the greater freedom he now had to teach dogmatics and New Testament exegesis. His secondary one-hour course was on eschatology.[2] The lectures on John are unique in this regard: When he had only reached 1:12 a former student gave to Eduard Thurneysen the enthusiastic report that Barth was even giving some instruction in philology.[3] Thurneysen passed on this verdict, commenting that Barth was now "in his tunnel," and in reply Barth stated that he was indeed deep in the tunnel of John, for some unknown spirit was impelling him to write out everything twice, which made it all much more vivid. He liked the bit about philology. This naive impression arose out of the fact that now, as he ought to have done long ago in Aargau and had gradually learned to do at Göttingen, he was drawing his new wisdom from the Greek concordance.[4] On January 17, 1926, Barth admitted to his friends that he had only reached ch. 4. People were

---

[1]Cf. K. Barth and E. Thurneysen, *Briefwechsel,* vol. 2 (1921-1930) (Zurich, 1974), Index pp. 741f.

[2]Ibid., p. 365.

[3]Ibid., p. 387.

[4]Ibid., p. 390.

cooperating enthusiastically, and if he now had a new smack of scholarship, this might be touching and encouraging but it did not avert his many fits of depression or his plans to retreat to a rural parish in Switzerland or something similar.[5] Three days later he told Thurneysen that he everywhere reached much the same results in expounding John. The only thing that surprised him was that the serpent in the wilderness made less impression on his friend than on himself. This animal, or its lifting up, seemed to him to be of great eschatological significance.[6] A most instructive letter is that which he sent to his brother Heinrich on January 30, 1926,[7] in which he told him about the lectures but said that unfortunately he was only at ch. 6 and would not finish by a long way.[8] He found it a most remarkable book. Often the whole room seemed to go round when he considered the ramifications of this chapter and found astonishing things that previous exegesis had missed. He thought it an advantage of theologians over philosophers that their studies are subject to canonical texts of this kind. He had no taste for the Johannine question or the answers to it. He constantly had his father's exposition by him.[9] His father thought it important that the son of Zebedee was the author, and if this was true, then the historical scandal was all the more unheard-of. It was odd that twenty or thirty years before this time people had not found it so, viewing it as settling rather than unsettling simply that an eyewitness had supposedly written all this. Barth did not know who it was, but he never ceased to be surprised at the fact.

In 1933, a year before his suspension, he was astonished to be asked to repeat the course at Bonn. This was due to a last-minute decision made on April 28 along with his colleague and neighbor, the New Testament scholar K. L. Schmidt, who, as Barth told the General Superintendent Stoltenhoff, had been forced to seek an academic permit for the semester, and had only just re-

---

[5]Ibid., pp. 396f.

[6]Ibid., p. 402, with a reference to Thurneysen's essay "Jesus und der Täufer (Johannes 3, 22-36)," Zwischen den Zeiten. 4 (1926), 102-134.

[7]In the Karl Barth archive at Basel, like all the letters that follow.

[8]Barth did not get beyond ch. 8.

[9]Barth had three handwritten lecture outlines by his father (Fritz Barth) that he never mentioned in the lectures: "Einführung in die Johanneische Frage" (1909), "Evangelium Johannis Cap. 1–17" (1893 and 1910), and "Praktische Erklärung ausgewählter Abschnitte des Johannesevangeliums" (1896).

ceived permission to ask for the permit, as Barth told Karl Stoevesandt the next day. So in addition to his lectures on the history
of Protestant theology, Barth offered the course on John, teaching
fourteen hours a week in all.[10] As he also told his brother Peter in
a letter dated May 18, 1933, in addition he had two seminars in
systematics and a homiletics class with 150 students,[11] so that he
was giving instruction in four disciplines. He also mentioned his
venture in practical theology to Heinrich Scholz in a letter dated
May 24, 1933. The description that Charlotte von Kirschbaum gave
Thurneysen supplies the background of Barth's activity; he was on
a powderkeg (or in the lions' den?). She expressed amazement that
his course thus far had been so smooth and that efforts from outside (e.g., by the German Christians) had not hurt his good rela-
tions with the students. Every morning, after Schleiermacher, he
gave his very important lectures on John to a large and attentive
audience; members of the Stahlhelm and Nazis sat there in their
uniforms (their caps on the walls), listening and taking notes. They
were there in more or less equal numbers in the Calvin seminar
and homiletics class as well, and heard things that really had very
little to do with the Third Reich. From a letter of Charlotte von
Kirschbaum to Barth's mother we gather that he repeated unaltered
the 1929 lectures on the history of theology, since he had no time
to rewrite them, especially as he had to correct and dictate those
on John's Gospel.

II

The 1925/1926 lectures — Text A in this edition — are extant in a
manuscript which Barth corrected and extensively revised in 1933
for Charlotte von Kirschbaum to type. The typescript — Text B — is
the basis of the present volume. Differences that are more than
stylistic are noted. Where A obviously makes better sense, it becomes the main text and B is given in the note. At times there
might be slips in typing (as on p. 153). In the few instances of
syntactical error or imperfection, the editor has emended the text,

---

[10]Schmidt remained a member of the Social Democratic party and might
have been dismissed or even imprisoned. He was later dismissed and was called
to a chair at Basel in 1935.

[11]Published under the title *Homiletik* (Zurich, 1966) [Eng. tr., *The Preaching of the Gospel* (Philadelphia, 1963)].

in which case the original is in the note, or he has supplied what is missing in brackets (as on p. 134). When appropriate, parts of quotations left out by Barth, or additions to quotations that he had made, are also in brackets (cf. p. 14 and p. 37).

The editor has added the biblical references in brackets. At times he has put more general allusions in footnotes (e.g., p. 140 and p. 146). Barth himself supplied all the other references. The editor has retained his common practice of putting these in parentheses when they are not part of the text.[12] He has used ff. instead of Barth's f., however, where there are more than two verses. Barth's distinctive spelling has also been retained even when it is not in the typescript, but the punctuation has been brought into line with the rules adopted for the *Gesamtausgabe.*

In the footnotes — there are none in A or B — the editor has documented the differences between the two editions and supplied missing references for quotations. In the main the works used by Barth (and still in his library) are cited. The notes show where he drew on secondary sources. Only rarely (p. 128 n. 188) does the editor point to other works.

In A Barth makes rich use of underlining. Little of this is reproduced in B, and the editor has done some selective italicizing in accordance with Barth's normal practice. To make for easier reading the editor has introduced breaks in what are often very long paragraphs. The dates of the lectures are indicated in the margin.[13] When not supplied in the typescript they are put in brackets; markings in the typescript offer the necessary guidance.

Thanks are due to Hinrich Stoevesandt and his wife for their unselfish, critical, and very helpful assistance in preparing this edition and compiling the Index of Subjects. Hannelotte Reiffen of Bonn rendered good service in deciphering manuscript A in relation to B. The Hermeneutical Institute of the Evangelical Theological Seminary of the University of Tübingen helped to make the Greek parts of the typescript legible for the compositor.

Bad Neuheim, October 31, 1976   Walther Fürst

---

[12]These have been omitted in the translation, however, when the editor has supplied the full reference in a footnote. — Trans.

[13]These dates have been omitted in the translation. — Trans.

INTRODUCTION

It must have been in February of 416 that Augustine, bishop of Hippo, began his famous 124 tractates on John's Gospel.[1] We might commence our own study of the same subject by a brief consideration of the thoughts with which the church father opens his treatment. In relation to John 1:1-5 he asks how his hearers are to understand, and how he is to state and explain what is written, when over both of them stands the judgment that the natural man does not understand the things of the Spirit of God [1 Cor. 2:14]. There is need to appeal for the assistance of grace. They must all understand what they can, and he must say what he can. For who can say it as it is? "I dare to say, brethren, that perhaps not even John himself has said it as it is, but only as he could, for a *man* has here spoken about God, a man enlightened by God, but still a man. (*Quia de Deo homo dixit et quidem inspiratus a Deo sed tamen homo.*) Because enlightened, he has said something; if he had not been enlightened, he could have said nothing; but because he is an enlightened *man*, he has not said it all as it is, but only said it as a man can say it."[2] Ps. 71:3 of the Latin Bible may be adduced here: *Suscipiant montes pacem populo tuo et colles ius-*

---

[1] *Tractatus in Ioannis Evangelium.* Barth uses the German version translated by T. Specht in *Bibliothek der Kirchenväter: des heiligen Kirchenvaters Aurelius Augustinus ausgewählte Schriften,* vol. IV (Kempten/Munich, 1913). The Latin in B is from J.-P. Migne, *Patrologia latina,* XXXV (St. Augustine III, 2), cols. 1379ff. [Cf. the English translation by J. Gibb and J. Innes in *St. Augustin: Homilies on the Gospel of John,* Nicene and Post-Nicene Fathers, ed. P. Schaff (repr. Grand Rapids, 1974), First Series, vol. VII, pp. 7-57.]

[2] Op. cit., I, 1 (pp. 1f.). [See Eng. tr. p. 7.]

titiam [= Eng. Ps. 72:3]. There are mountains and hills in relation
to what we receive from God, i.e., greater and smaller souls. The
former are enlightened by wisdom, receive peace, and impart it to
the latter that these may live by their faith. From the mountains it
is said to the church: Peace be with you. One of these high mountains who received peace on behalf of the hills (the rest of us) was
John the Evangelist. But even as a high mountain John is still one
of those of whom it is said that no eye has seen, nor ear heard, nor
has it entered into any human heart [1 Cor. 2:9]. If wisdom came
into the heart of John, then it was only insofar as he was not a man
but had begun to be an angel, i.e., one who proclaims God, only
insofar as God called him and he mounted with his heart above all
created things and met the Word by whom all things were created.
But not to be a man in this sense, to be instead one who is called
to proclaim God, presupposes that he is first known and acknowledged precisely in his humanity. In relation to the Evangelist, then,
we have to recall not only: "I lift up mine eyes to the hills, from
whence cometh my help" [Ps. 121:1] (although in truth he stands
high and holy among all the mountains which have received peace
for the people of God), but also the continuation of Ps. 121: "My
help is from the Lord, who hath made heaven and earth" [v. 2].
Hence "lift up your eyes to this mountain, i.e., the Evangelist."[3]
But "do not lift up your eyes to this mountain in such a way that
you think you must set your hope on a man."[4] "The mountains
receive only what they pass on to us; it is to the place from which
they themselves receive it that we are to direct our hope[5] (*unde et
montes accipiunt, ibi spes nostra ponenda est*)." "If we lift our eyes
to the scriptures because these are given to us by men, we lift our
eyes to the mountains from which help comes to us; but because
those who wrote the scriptures were also men, they do not shine
of themselves, but *he* was the true light that enlightens[6] everyone
that comes into this world." It is precisely in this sense that the
other John, the Baptist, says of himself: I am not the Christ, and:
Of his fulness have we all received. What the mountains impart to
us is the possibility of hearing something. They cannot impart the

---

[3]Op. cit., I, 6 (p. 5). [See Eng. tr. p. 8.]
[4]Loc. cit. [See Eng. tr. p. 8.]
[5]Loc. cit. [See Eng. tr. pp. 8f.]
[6]Loc. cit. The original has "who enlightens." [See Eng. tr. p. 9.]

illumination of the understanding. They themselves need illumination. John the Evangelist "offered words, but thou must receive understanding where he who offers thee the words attained it,[7] that thou mayest thus lift up thine eyes to the hills from whence thy help comes, and there receive the cup, i.e., the Word, that is held out to thee, yet still (because thy help is from the Lord who made heaven and earth) fill thy heart at the place where he also filled it."[8] The hearers should thus see that their preacher is only apparently nearer to them than God. "Direct your ears to me and your hearts to him." "See, you lift your eyes and your bodily senses to us, and yet not to us (for we are not among the mountains) but to the Gospel, to the Evangelist, and your heart, that is to be filled, to the Lord."[9] Let each of us see to the heart and whither it is lifted up. "If one sees that one bears the burden of the flesh, one takes pains to purify by continence what one lifts up to God."[10] Blessed are the pure in heart, for they shall see God [Matt. 5:3].

Thus far Augustine's introduction. I have quoted it because it reminds us that as we face the task of reading and explaining John's Gospel, we enter a concrete, specific situation whose form does not depend at all on us but which is this situation and not another by a necessity that lies in the matter itself. What kind of a situation is it? With the help of what we have just heard, I would point to three decisive features.

1. We cannot open and read the Gospel without first realizing that it comes to us as the "good news," as its title indicates, that the Word of wisdom which the Evangelist passes on (not as it is but as he could) is spoken to us, that the "cup" of divine, i.e., new and unheard-of, truth that challenges all our other knowledge does in fact reach us so that the question of faith is put to us. No matter what our answer may be, no matter that we must all see ourselves as natural beings who do not understand the things of the Spirit of God [cf. 1 Cor. 2:14]! It is not in dispute that we are hills which hear of divine peace from the mountain. The Gospel is the mountain from which that peace comes to the hills. We hear (and understand)

---

[7]A: "where he also drank that offers to thee" (Specht's translation). In B, then, Barth corrected the translation of Specht that he used in A.

[8]Op. cit., I, 7 (p. 6). [See Eng. tr. p. 9.]

[9]Op. cit., I, 7 (p. 7). [See Eng. tr. p. 9.]

[10]Ibid.

the Gospel only when we do not ignore that relation between it and us, when we do not ignore the actuality or reality with which it does not so much stand over against us as encounter us. We cannot adduce any objections based on the usual rights of scholarship.[11] We cannot ignore that relation. In it and in it alone the Gospel is what it is and seeks to be studied as such inasmuch as it is a subject of scholarship. If we ignore that relation, then with the same reason or unreason we might study wooden iron or frozen fire. If the Gospel, John's Gospel, is not directed to us in the name of God and does not presuppose and demand our faith — then what else can we say of it but that it is a fantasy no matter how truly it might be before us on paper in what is probably its earliest text? If it is simply the monument of no more than a historical entity, if it is dumb or a Word that is or was directed to others — no matter what else it may be,[12] it is not the Gospel, it is not John's Gospel. The true Gospel of John that we have to study can be only the Gospel of John that comes to us. How do we know this?

How is it that Augustine assumes from the very first lines that John's Gospel is necessarily speaking to him and to his listeners? Certainly not because of some so-called subjective presupposition. Conscientious expositors must be as free as possible from such things as religious or non-religious notions, from philosophical or ethical convictions, from personal feelings or reactions, from historical habits of thought, prejudices, and the like. They must have an ear simply for what the text says to them, for the new thing that it seeks to say in face of the totality of their previous subjective knowledge. This freedom is part of the lifting up of the heart about which Augustine goes on to speak. If we want to be truly objective readers and expositors of John's Gospel, however, we will not want to free ourselves from the fact that we are baptized, that for us, then, John's Gospel is part of the canonical scripture of the Christian church. It was not written and does not exist as anything other. Canonical scripture, however, means scripture to which we stand in that relation from the very first,[13] a Word that is spoken to us from the very first in the name of God and

---

[11]A adds "(naturally in the interests of scholarship itself)."

[12]A: "it is some kind of phantom, but."

[13]A uses *Relation* (B *Beziehung*) and adds "a priori in the strict sense of the term" after "from the very first."

with the claim that it is saying something radically new, a Word which even before we could hear it has opened a dialogue with us, a dialogue which, because it is conducted in the name of God,[14] we cannot escape. "From the very first," I say and therefore not on the basis or in the form of ordinary experience, nor on the basis or in the form of our faith, but on the basis and in the form of our life in the church of Christ as baptism attests to it. As we recall this life of ours under the sign of baptism and therefore in the sphere of the church of Christ, we do not indulge in the kind of presuppositions that we have to suspend or repress (perhaps at least provisionally) for the sake of the scientific investigation of a matter, as though the character of the Gospel as an authoritative address were perhaps[15] based on our apprehension or experience of its content; as though we stood in some better relation to the Gospel (e.g., by way of our own observation, reflection, or experience), as though fundamentally it could be told us in some other way than in the strict form of that "from the very first" in which it is told us in our baptism; as though the fact that we are baptized and in the Christian church were not originally and inescapably related to the witness of the prophets and apostles to the revelation of God, and hence to the true Gospel of John that applies to us. What does the church mean, or baptism, or God, if we have the possibility, if we can even reckon with the possibility, of abstracting away from it, of suspending our life in this nexus — if this presupposition is not validly grounded in an objectivity compared to which all other objectivity, e.g., historical objectivity, can be regarded only as a secondary, derived, or loaned objectivity?

2. It is, of course, part of the concrete specificity of the situation in which we find ourselves regarding the Gospel — and Augustine, as we have seen, laid great stress on this — that the Evangelist who addresses us in the name of God is a man. This does not alter the fact that the mountain is here speaking to the

---

[14]A: "because it concerns our existence, because we are called into question by it."

[15]After "in the church of Christ," A goes on as follows: "We should have a poor and weak concept of the church and sacrament if we were to object that this is a purely subjective presupposition, that we should (perhaps provisionally at least) suspend or suppress it for the sake of an objective experience of the matter, as though the character of the Gospel as an authoritative address were perhaps."

hills (and we are not among the mountains).[16] Not just anyone speaks to us, but a great soul,[17] and not just any great soul, but one who is called and enlightened, an apostle, one of those who wrote the scriptures that are called such in a qualified sense, one to whom wisdom is assigned in a very special way so that he may speak of it in a very special way to us. Hence, lift yourselves up to the Evangelist.[18] For the relation to him is in fact the relation in which wisdom imparts itself to us. Yet he is still a man. His historicity, to which we must cling, has a place and therefore a limit in time. It shares in the relativity, the specificity, and the questionability of every historical phenomenon. This entails a reservation. He is *only* a man. He has not said it as it *is* but as he could.[19] As we hear and understand his words we are wholly entangled in the historical problems that surround all human words. We cannot avoid them. We should not try. He is not Christ but John. He does not shine of or through himself. If we look at him we look into the darkness of history and not into the light. He passes on a light that he has himself received. But he only passes it on; the giver is he from whom he himself received it. It was as the recipient of that which the natural man does not grasp that he was no man but an angel, one who proclaims God. We may not, then, set our hope on him. He is not an apostle at the level of the historical phenomenon to which we are referred. On earth he bears no halo by which we know that he is an apostle as we know a king on his throne. To see him as an apostle we need the same illumination that he needed and received in order to be an apostle. He does not proclaim God without God, nor may he be known as one who proclaims God without God. His word is qualified as address in the sense described, as holy scripture, in virtue of God's address to us by means of the words of this man. We have to speak, not of quality, nor of the qualified nature, but of the qualifying of his word, not of a being but of an action, the divine action in virtue of which his word is qualified as address. That the Gospel really comes to us in that original and inescapable way is not proper to it as a kind of natural or magical force that may be perceived and experienced in the

---

[16]Cf. n. 9.
[17]Augustine, op. cit., I, 2 (p. 2). [See Eng. tr. p. 7.]
[18]Cf. n. 3.
[19]Cf. n. 2.

power of the reader, and displayed and made efficacious in the power of the preacher or exegete.

The Gospel comes to us with the promise that God himself will confess it. But it is not self-evident that this should happen. It is in the balances, no, it depends on God's good pleasure whether it does so or not. If it does not, we shall hear the Evangelist and yet not hear him. Thus our relation to him has a twofold character. We are pleased to let ourselves be bound by his word even as and although we see that in the first instance we have to do with it alone, with this particular man and his particular words in their own place, within the limit of his time, in all the specificity with which he speaks as a man like any other. We face a historical problem. But we let ourselves be bound only in order that, thus bound, we may be freed by God himself to and for God himself. Without being bound we cannot be freed, for it is from the mountains that the light comes to us, the little hills, from the apostles that the Word of God comes to those that are in the church. This is why we hear them and lift up our eyes to the hills. But without the liberation we are not bound, for the mountains do not illumine unless they are illumined, the apostles do not speak to us as such unless it is ever and again given to them to do so by God. Thus our help comes from the Lord who has made heaven and earth [Ps. 121:2]. As a medium[20] what is historical, the human word of the witness to revelation, demands our total, concentrated, and serious attention. But only as a medium,[21] not for its own sake and not to be understood in terms of itself, but as witness which itself needs witness and expects witness — the witness that its subject must give. This giving is an event, an action, the action of God in the strictest sense of the term. The point of our own action as hearers and expositors of the Gospel stands or falls with God's action through the instrument with which we have to do.

3. Our situation as readers and expositors of the Gospel means finally that we are placed under a specific demand. This relates to our own concrete attitude to this task. I do not mean the demand for faith. Our starting point is that the Gospel at once addresses to us a demand for faith that we can neither miss nor avoid. I add that every point at which we are occupied with the Gospel carries

---

[20]A adds "as a transparency."
[21]A: "as a *medium*, as a *transparency.*"

this demand with it and necessarily has the significance of an act of obedience or disobedience to this demand. But what is faith if not the illumination without which we cannot perceive the light of scripture? And what is this illumination if not the inscrutable and uncontrollable work of God upon us for which we can only pray?[22] What we have now to discuss, however, is the other demand that Augustine expresses in connection with the familiar cultic formula of the early church: "Lift up your hearts."[23] What does this mean? If we listen to Augustine, the mysticism of Neoplatonism and the asceticism of the Hellenistic mystery religions tell us what he meant. From the mountains that we see with our eyes we should mount up higher and higher to the invisible One who has made the visible mountains, just as John as a recipient of the divine gift was one of the highest mountains because he rose up above everything created, above all heavens and angels, to the uncreated Word that was in the beginning. And for our hearts to be able to do this, they need cleansing — for they are carnal — they need the catharsis, the purifying of continence. To us these are alien notes. But they cannot be totally or finally alien. Alongside or prior to the faith that is not put in our own hands, on the level of what we desire and can do, in a way that does not bind him from whom every good gift comes, but not on that account without significance, there is a readiness for faith or for understanding what faith and its object are all about. Concretely, there is a readiness to understand[24] that only in the sphere denoted by the terms church, sacrament, and canon can John's Gospel be read and understood as the word of an apostle, i.e., as the word of a witness not to himself, but to the revelation imparted and entrusted to him. There is a readiness to look in the direction indicated, even if only in the form of a hypothetical intention demanded by an understanding of the formal nature of the subject.[25] There is an openness to the need to understand this matter within its own logic and ethic. There is a willingness to

---

[22]After "upon us" A inserts: "Hence this demand stands under the sign of the other Augustinian saying: 'Give what thou commandest.' "

[23]Barth has in view the *sursum corda* of the Roman mass.

[24]A has "for the understanding."

[25]A: "to look in the direction indicated, to set oneself in that place, even if only (should one think one can or should personally reject the faith demanded) in the form of a hypothetical intention demanded by the subject."

adapt to this need because one wants to understand. Instead of willingness, then, we might say objectivity. We are perhaps not guilty of too great misrepresentation if we go on to say that the continence that Augustine commends consists concretely of opposing to the subjective presuppositions with which, to the hurt of our understanding, we constantly approach scripture, the equally subjective but sincere and earnest desire to read and expound the Gospel, not as teachers but as students, not as those who know but as those who do not know, as those who let ourselves be told[26] what the Gospel, and through it the divine wisdom, is seeking to tell us, holding ourselves free for it as for a message that we have never heard before. This readiness can be the subject of a demand. We can want it, seek it, and have it. It is not a final word. It is not identical with faith. But as a penultimate word the demand for this readiness has its place. In the situation in which we find ourselves, as an integral part of its reality, there sounds forth unmistakably for all who are in it the cry: Lift up your hearts.

---

[26]A adds: "(over against ourselves!)."

VERSES 1-18

Augustine's exordium and my commentary upon it might just as well introduce the exposition of any other book of the New Testament rather than John's Gospel. That text reminds us of the basic elements in general biblical hermeneutics. Yet we have only to cast a glance at the first and clearly discernible section of the Gospel, its famous prologue in 1:1-18, to realize that it was neither by accident nor caprice that Augustine made his remarks in this context, and that with the apparently general considerations that we have appended to them we have in fact already approached our first, specific, and immediate exegetical task, namely, the exposition of the prologue.

*In the beginning was the Word, and the Word was with God, and God was the Word. He was in the beginning with God. Everything was made by him, and without him **nothing** that is was made. In him was life, and this life was the light of men. And the light shines in the darkness, and the darkness has not comprehended it.*

There was a man sent from God who was called John. He came for witness, to bear witness to the light, that all might come to faith through him. He was not the light but bore witness to the light.

He was coming into the world as the true light that lightens everyone. He was in the world, and the world was made by him, and the world knew him not. He came to his own home and his own people did not receive him. But those who did receive him, to them he gave the power[1] to become the children of God, even to

---

[1]A: "the possibility."

11

those who believed in his name. These were not born of blood, nor
of the will of the flesh, nor of the will of a man, but of God.

And the Word became flesh and dwelt among us, and we
beheld his glory, a glory as[2] *of an only-begotten of his Father, of*
one who is full of grace and truth. John bears witness to him, and
cries, and says: This was he of whom I said, he who comes after
me surpasses me, for he was above me from the very first. Of his
fulness we have all received grace for grace. The law was given by
Moses, but grace and truth are through Jesus Christ. No one has
ever seen God, but the only-begotten, God, who is in the bosom of
the Father, he has manifested him.

In support of the statement that our introductory discussion
of Augustine has led us on to the right track for an understanding
of the prologue, I might make the general observation that in the
prologue, too, there is a concern to make it clear to readers of the
Gospel that they are in a specific situation in relation to it, that
they are in some sense from the very first its prisoners. A word,
no, *the* Word has been spoken which in principle, as the Word of
the Creator, precedes and is superior to all that is (vv. 1-3). A light
shines, namely, the life that was originally in the Word. It shines
in the darkness for all people. It has always shone. It was in the
world (vv. 4-5, 9-10). All people are from the very first *hoi idioi,*
his own people (v. 11). It may be that they are darkness that does
not comprehend the light (v. 5), cosmos that does not know it
(v. 10), people who do not receive their Lord (v. 11). But this does
not alter the fact that the light shines in the darkness (v. 5), that
the world was made by him who is the light (vv. 3, 10), that these
are from the very first his own people (v. 11). The dice have been
cast concerning humanity once the Evangelist, even though he, too,
is only a man, introduces his theme. He omits the *sursum corda,*
the express appeal to readers with which Augustine finally brings
to light the significance of the situation. He was able to omit it. For
who will not hear it at the end of the prologue, unspoken though
it is?

Nevertheless, there is a more specific relation between the
thoughts of Augustine and the Johannine prologue. Those who have
studied John's Gospel more closely know what is the exegetical

---

[2]A has *wie* here, B *als.*

crux of the prologue. It is concrete and palpable in vv. 6-8 and
v. 15. These verses deal with a John, John the Baptist, as is plain
in the rest of the chapter. They tell us that the author wants to
show us at once what is the relation of this John to the Word, to
the light about which vv. 1-5 and vv. 9-13 speak, to the incarnate
Word that is seen by us (v. 14), to Jesus Christ, as will at last be
openly stated in v. 17. He, this John, is not himself this Word; he
is a man sent by God (v. 6). He is not himself the light; he is a
witness to it (v. 8). He bears witness that the one who comes after
him surpasses him, as he is before him in principle (v. 8). But v. 7
makes the same point in a positive way. He, this John, has come to
bear witness to the light that all might come to faith through him.

There can be no question but that these four verses, above
all, cause difficulty to readers and expositors. Vv. 6-8 and v. 15
constitute an interruption which we should like to expunge in the
interests of a smoother reading. If they were not there, then for all
the other obscurities and ambiguities, understanding the prologue
would be a relatively simple task. But they are in fact there, and
there can be no doubt but that it is they that give the prologue the
concrete appearance with which we have to reckon. They are important. The author has an urgent concern to say what they say.
This is true even if, as Bultmann has assumed,[3] they are to be
viewed as marginal corrections or strengthenings which the author
added to an older work that he adopted and revised. He certainly
did not want to see the prologue go out and be read without these
verses. In their concreteness, and materially in their significant
relation to the real beginning of the Gospel in v. 19, they stand out
strangely from the verses around them, and precisely in so doing
they bring to light the practical purpose of the introductory statement. Whatever we may think about this purpose, whatever view
we may take of the literary relation of these verses to the verses
around them, whatever may be our position vis-à-vis the textual
and historical[4] questions raised by these verses, one thing is cer-

---

[3]R. Bultmann, "Der religionsgeschichtliche Hintergrund des Prologs zum
Johannes-Evangelium," in *Eucharistêrion. Studien zur Religion und Literatur des
Alten und Neuen Testaments, Hermann Gunkel zum 60 Geburtstag,* Part 2 (Göttingen, 1923), pp. 3-26, esp. p. 24; repr. in *Exegetica. Aufsätze zur Erforschung
des Neuen Testaments,* ed. E. Dinkler (Tübingen, 1967), pp. 10-35, esp. p. 33.

[4]A has *religionsgeschichtlichen und literarkritischen.*

tain, namely, that the problem of the relation between revelation and the witness to revelation, which is the issue in Augustine's exordium, is precisely what the author undoubtedly wanted to pinpoint in these verses (and not, perhaps, in these verses alone), his aim being to make readers of the Gospel aware of their situation and to put them in the right place in this situation.

He is speaking about *John the Baptist* as a witness to revelation. But only later, after the prologue, does he make this express distinction even though he, the author, is also called John, or wants to be called John, or is supposed to be called John according to the tradition. As though it did not matter much if there is a temporary confusion between the two Johns in the minds of readers, as though such a confusion or conflation might even be welcome, he first leaves a certain haziness around the name John which he removes only later. We follow a clue first noted by Franz Overbeck[5] when we stress the remarkable proximity of the two Johns in the mind of the author. According to Overbeck this answers the question why the author wanted to be called John or to rely on the authority of John. Overbeck believed that in relation to Jesus the apostle John serves[6] as another witness alongside the Baptist John. "As the Baptist is the witness of the Logos, the mediator between him and the world prior to the completion of his epiphany in the world, before the Logos is at the point of perfectly showing the world [by][7] himself the glory of God on earth, so John the apostle is the mediator for the Logos after his departure from the world." "He is called John on account of his calling in the Gospel and the inner relationship of this calling to that of the Baptist in the whole economy of the divine light in the world according to the basic conception of this economy on which the whole of the Fourth Gospel rests according to the prologue" (p. 417).

As for the narrower issue of the name in the Fourth Gospel, one might question this hypothesis and still not affect the excellence of the observation on which it rests. There is in fact an inner relationship of calling between the two Johns. There is also perhaps — I am less certain of this — a parallelism, as Overbeck

---

[5]F. Overbeck, *Das Johannesevangelium. Studien zur Kritik seiner Erforschung.* ed. C. A. Bernoulli (Tübingen, 1911), pp. 416f.

[6]A has *gilt* for *dient,* i.e., "counts" instead of "serves."

[7]An addition by Barth.

suggests, between the witness before and the witness after. One certainly cannot say that the Fourth Evangelist has only a negative or polemical interest in the one who bears his name. Note that in contrast to the Synoptists he is not content to assign to the Baptist merely the position of a forerunner in the sense of a prophet who simply predicts the Messiah, of one who proclaims him that is to come. No, with *houtos ēn* he at once stresses the Baptist's word of witness (v. 15). He has him bear express witness to the one who has already come (vv. 26, 29ff., and then again in 3:27ff.). He is the first to point to the one who was then living unrecognized in the midst of Israel before there was ever a disciple or an "apostle" insofar as this word is to be distinguished from the term prophet. Note also that as compared with the Synoptics the Fourth Gospel enhances, as it were, the position of the Baptist by understanding and interpreting his function of preaching repentance and remission in direct reference to Jesus and claiming his baptism directly as Christian baptism (Overbeck, p. 419). The statement of Walter Bauer[8] that the attitude of the Evangelist to the Baptist and his followers is to be regarded as one of "intentional contradiction" can hardly be viewed as a happy one in the light of these theses. But there is more. The Baptist is the man who in v. 32 bears witness to the descent of the Spirit upon Jesus from heaven. If the Evangelist now bears witness also to Jesus and his mission, he is not therewith opening a new, let alone an opposing, series. He is placing himself in the series that opens already with John the Baptist. To be sure, he is critical in relation to the Baptist. He shows reserve. He makes distinction. He sets him in his place. Yet we do not find criticism alone. Or, one might say, the criticism is positive. It is also — inevitably — criticism of himself in the same series. If the assumption is correct that according to the author's intention we are to find in the unnamed disciple among those mentioned in v. 35 and v. 40 either the author himself or the one who vouches authoritatively for him, the one in whose name he speaks, then with the ambivalence that is fitting in this matter he is stating that the Baptist was his first teacher, his human master, through whose witness: "Behold, this is the Lamb of God" (v. 36), he was led to

[8]W. Bauer, *Das Johannesevangelium*. Lietzmann Handbuch zum Neuen Testament, vol. 6, 2nd ed. (Tübingen, 1925), p. 14.

the eternal Word and light, to Jesus. By way of the Baptist he introduces himself, and he is at once on the most significant path to Jesus. And is he doing anything other, in writing the Gospel, than what this teacher of his has done? Does he have this teacher say anything less in v. 29, and especially in 3:35-36, than the sum of his own Gospel? Does he call himself, or his companions in 15:27, or the author, his later editor of 21:24, anything greater than simply a *martyrōn*, precisely as John the Baptist was? "I have greater witness than that of John," says Christ in 5:36, but not his disciple! Often in the Gospel the words of Jesus as the incarnate Word are called *martyrein* or *martyria*. This fact obviously illuminates the relative dignity of him who in the prologue is called a mere witness, but who is set in contrast as such. Is it not noteworthy and significant, even if exegetically mistaken, that the entire exposition of the early church regarded vv. 16-18 as a continuation of v. 15, and therefore as the words of the Baptist rather than the words of the Evangelist, and that they could do so, things being as ambivalent as they are, with a claim to no little probability? What support have we even in v. 14 for excluding the Baptist from the *hēmeis* that is presupposed in the *etheasametha*? No, there is proximity or solidarity here. In Overbeck's phrase, there is here an "inner relationship of calling." In John the Baptist John the Evangelist — no matter how this may relate to the question of the name of the Gospel — recognizes and understands himself as well, and his own problematical status. Aware that I am probably trying to say something too precise to do justice to the complex material, but seeking to point in the direction in which, as I see it, the real significance lies, I might venture the paradox that John the Evangelist is wrestling with himself when he wrestles with John the Baptist; with himself, i.e., with his existence and function as the human witness who stands between revelation and humanity. He instructs his readers concerning his own relation to this subject when in the same context he instructs them concerning John the Baptist. He wants to make it clear what he, the Evangelist, does and does not do as such, what he can do and cannot do, what he is and is not. He does this by means of the one who for himself and his contemporaries is the great and most significant paradigm of the concept of the "witness," namely, the figure of the Baptist.

Within this view, if the presuppositions are correct, there

might be truth in all that Richard Reitzenstein[9] and others, along
the lines of the history of religion, say about the possible ecclesiastical significance of the treatment of the Baptist in the prologue
and in the Gospel as a whole. It might well be that what is reckoned
with here is a competing religion which goes back to a chronologically indeterminate form[10] of Mandean thinking and which honors
the Baptist as the revealer. In the last resort this theory might shed
an interesting light on the problem of the genesis of the Johannine
prologue. The troublesome phenomenon of a Baptist sect would
then have provided the Evangelist with the occasion for bringing
the prologue to this concrete climax. Yet in this very case too his
own problem (and perhaps even his own biographical problem)
would in fact have motivated him. And obviously this would have
been a serious enough material problem for him to unfold it at the
outset of the Gospel with a solemnity which ill accords with the
almost complete disappearance of the question of the Baptist after
ch. 3 if in fact the issue is merely one of ecclesiastical politics, of
the Baptist sect. W. Bauer (op. cit., p. 14) undoubtedly claims far
too much when he says that the depiction of the relation between
Jesus and John is to be regarded "only as a practical one," i.e., as
a polemic against the Baptist sect. It is certainly practical in this
very concrete sense but it is not only practical! I would rather say
that through the transparency of what might have been a historical
and ecclesiastical situation the author is speaking about the situation which arises, or is already present, when someone other than
Christ himself, a man, but an authorized man, an *anthrōpos apestalmenos para theou* (v. 6), speaks about Christ. He is speaking
about the claim and authority with which this necessarily takes
place (cf. v. 7 with the unquestionable word of the editor in 21:24),
but also about the danger of confusion that can arise, and therefore
about the required criticism with which such a man must be dif-
ferentiated from the one about whom he speaks. We find in 5:35
the complaint against the Jews that he, John the Baptist, was a
burning and shining light but they were willing to rejoice in his
transitory human light (*agalliasthēnai pros hōran en tǭ phōti*)

---

[9]Cf. R. Reitzenstein, *Das iranische Erlösungsmysterium. Religionsgeschichtliche Untersuchungen* (Bonn, 1921).
    [10]A: "pre-Christian form" (*vorchristliche Mandäertum*).

(Overbeck, p. 420). This is precisely what should not happen in
the relationship of revealer, witness, and hearers that the Baptist
typifies.

If the above observations are all correct, then Augustine's
exordium is not so remote from the text as it might seem to be at
first glance. The Johannine prologue is not dealing with the general situation of humanity vis-à-vis revelation. It is dealing concretely with the question of the situation that arises when we hear
a witness to revelation, when we lift up our eyes to the hills from
which our help comes, and yet when we can expect help only from
the Lord who made heaven and earth. All this casts at once a
brilliant light on the distinctively radical way in which the Evangelist approaches his task. He knows what he is doing when he
sets about the work. He is concerned to express this, to see to it
that the place from which he speaks, from which he confronts his
readers, is depicted both positively and negatively. As he perhaps
in fact brings to light the hopeless confusion of witness and revealer
of which that competing religion might have been guilty, as he
honors the witness and yet draws the line by calling him a witness,
he sets himself in his own place and his readers in theirs. More
plainly than anywhere else in the Bible except in the parallel 1 John
1–4, which is probably by the same author or from the same circle,
we are told here what the Bible is, namely, witness to revelation
both in relation to revelation and yet also in distinction from it.
What might at first seem to be exegetically very remote in the
passage from Augustine is in fact typically Johannine. There is said
in it by way of introduction something which has to be said by way
of introduction to the exposition of all biblical books as such: the
great Yes and No with which these books call us to themselves only
to point us to the Lord, as the Baptist pointed his disciples. This
is the radical procedure of the Gospel, or at least a distinctive
example of it. For we have the prologue only in the light of what
I have called his practical intention. I have anticipated because, led
on the one side by Augustine and on the other by the present state
of the religio-historical and literary-critical debate, I incline to the
opinion that if in the total web of the prologue we lay hold of this
one thread, we shall in fact find the guiding thread to an understanding of its content as a whole. The radius of the circle that this
section draws is naturally much larger than has been expressed in
our deliberations thus far. The question, or rather the answer, the

insight with which the Evangelist approaches his task, is obviously
not exhausted by his formula for the relation between Christ and
John, between revelation and its witness. Nevertheless, one might
say, and only in this light does the exordium of Augustine commend
itself, that in the framework of a much more comprehensive consideration the purpose of the prologue achieves in that formula its
most concrete form.

We shall now turn to the detailed exegesis of what must be
regarded as the much more comprehensive material.

1. En archę ēn ho logos. The order of the sentence lays the
stress on *en archę*. It is correct to translate: "In the beginning was
the Word," but the usual emphasis on "the Word," though what it
may seem to be saying sounds profound, is not in keeping with the
meaning of the statement. *What* was in the beginning, namely, the
Word and not something else, is not the point here. Instead, something is being said about the Word. It was already *in the beginning.*
It did not come into being or arise subsequently.[11] *En archę, in
principio* (Vulgate), in unmistakable allusion to Gen. 1:1, denotes
the beginning of all being as it is posited by divine creation. The
world that is distinct from God enters into existence *en archę*. The
Logos also was *en archę*. This does not mean that the Logos itself
is this *archē*. As may be seen from what follows, it does not belong
to the world that is distinct from God, not even as its beginning,
not even as the first and oldest link in the chain of created things.
This, of course, is how Philo understood it: *presbytatos tōn genesin
eilēphotōn* (W. Bauer, op. cit., p. 9). And this was how Prov. 8:22
viewed divine wisdom: *kyrios ektisen me archēn hodōn autou.*
When it is said here that the Logos was *en archę*, it is distinguished
from the beginning of the created world and therefore from this
world itself. The same is true of the *ap' archēs* that is used in the
parallel 1 John 1:1 and also of the remarkable *prōtotokos pasēs
ktiseōs* of Col. 1:12. The Logos was in, with, before, and above the
totality of the created world. There is no space in this world that
is not limited by it. There is no possibility of evading or escaping
it; no more than of evading or escaping God himself. That "the
Logos was in the beginning" means that he is as God. Only God,
the Creator himself, was "in the beginning." That he "was" in the

---

[11] The different text of A begins here; see n. 13.

beginning means that he is beyond the coming into being of what arises with the beginning. By him, in virtue of his being, there is a coming into being (v. 3). His being as such is not one that comes into being. It is not temporal; it is the eternal being that in principle precedes and encloses and originates all time. The Athanasians of the fourth century were right when they based on this *ēn* their thesis that there was no time in which the Logos was not.[12] The text means precisely that the Logos was before all time.[13]

But how can there be a being in the beginning apart from and alongside the being of God? The first statement suggests this question, and the second statement answers it: *kai ho logos ēn pros ton theon*. There is no need to switch subject and predicate in this case. The natural stress undoubtedly falls on the *pros ton theon*. The saying is a statement about the Word; it was *with God*. No one was in the beginning (v. 1) apart from or alongside God. But the Word was not apart from or alongside God. The Word was "with God." It belonged to God. The translation of Heinrich Holtzmann:

---

[12]Cf. R. Seeberg, *Lehrbuch der Dogmengeschichte*, vol. 2, 3rd ed. (Erlangen/Leipzig, 1923), p. 95.

[13]A: The word *archē* is to be translated "beginning," not "origin." The allusion to Gen. 1:1 is unmistakable. The beginning of all being, of all that is, is the issue. The Logos, the Word, was in the same beginning as God was when he created. He was *in initio*. Note that it does not say that the beginning was the Word. Because the beginning (and this is why we are to avoid the rendering "origin") is the beginning of the world (not the divine beginning as such), then if it were hypostatized and equated with the Logos, the Logos would logically have to be understood as the first and oldest link that opens the chain of created things. This is the case in Philo. In him the Logos *is* the beginning, namely, as *presbytatos tōn genesin eilēphotōn* (W. Bauer, op. cit., p. 9). What Prov. 8:22 says about the divine sophia points in the same direction: *kyrios ektisen me archēn hodōn autou*. But here the Logos is not said to be *hē archē*. The greater thing is said that the Logos was *en archę̄, in* the beginning, simultaneously with the beginning, distinct from the beginning of created things. One has to say that the expression has the advantage of greater precision over *ap' archēs* in the parallel 1 John 1:1. The Logos was where, according to Gen. 1:1, only the Creator himself could be outside the world that is beginning. He was, *ēn*, beyond all *egeneto*. He who is distinct from the beginning of all things is obviously distinct also from the beginning of time. *In initio* has to mean *in initio temporis*. His being is not temporal; it is eternal being that in principle precedes all time and encloses all time. The Athanasians were right when they based on this passage their thesis that there was no time in which the Logos was not. In fact John means that the Logos was, in principle, *before* all time. This is what *en archę̄ ēn* has to mean here.

"It was toward God,"[14] is right in suggesting relationship but it is still misleading. W. Bauer correctly abandoned this translation and explanation. *Ad te nos creasti,* as Augustine puts it in a famous passage,[15] obviously fits the creature, especially the human creature, but not an entity that is to be sought beyond the *archē.* That the Word was *ad Deum* would not be an answer to the question how far it was what only God can be, namely, *en archę.* The idea of Theodor Zahn[16] about the intercourse with God or movement toward God in which the Logos was involved also leads us astray. The reason is the same; a being that was not *en archę* might also have dealings with God. *Pros ton theon* has to define a being that was *en archę.* It has to explain how it could be this. W. Bauer was right when he took *pros* to mean "with" with no nuances. The statement forms what is, of course, the paradoxical answer to the question who could be *en archę* outside and alongside God. The answer is that he could be this who was with God, who, belonging to God, with God, being after the manner of God, stood and essentially stands beyond the line that is drawn by the beginning of all things. The Word was "with God" — therefore it was in the beginning.

But how could it be *pros ton theon,* or belong to God? The third statement gives the answer: *kai theos ēn ho logos.* If in the first two sentences we were right to put the stress on the statements made about the Logos, we may assume that the situation is the same in the third sentence, that we must once again reverse the statement, that we have to recognize in *theos,* even though it comes first, the predicate (cf. 4:24: *pneuma ho theos*), that this is where the emphasis lies, that the Logos was God, i.e., of divine nature or essence. It has rightly been pointed out that the predicate that is here ascribed to the Logos is *theos,* not *ho theos.* But it is doubtful whether one does well to follow W. Bauer (op cit., p. 10) in recalling

---

[14]H. J. Holtzmann, *Evangelium des Johannes.* 3, rev. ed. W. Bauer, Hand-Commentar zum Neuen Testament, vol. 4 (Tübingen, 1908), p. 32.

[15]Augustine, *Confessiones* I, 1, 1: *Fecisti nos ad te, et inquietum est cor nostrum, donec requiescat in te.* [See the English translation by J. G. Pilkington in *The Confessions and Letters of St. Augustine,* Nicene and Post-Nicene Fathers, vol. I (repr. Grand Rapids, 1974), p. 45: "Thou hast formed us for Thyself, and our hearts are restless till they find rest in Thee."

[16]T. Zahn, *Das Evangelium des Johannes.* Kommentar zum Neuen Testament, vol. IV, 5 and 6, corrected and enlarged ed. (Leipzig/Erlangen, 1921), p. 49.

the loose, improper use with which Philo calls the Logos *theos*, or
to think with Theodor Zahn of the occasional way in which *ha'
elohim* in the OT is not a proper name but is used for a category,
e.g., spirits, angels, or even men. At any rate, we are advised to
treat with caution the usual inference that the Logos is not here
identified with God. A distinction must be made. The nature of the
Logos is here identified with the nature of the entity called *ho theos*.
The *theotēs* of this entity is unreservedly ascribed to the Logos.
Significantly, the *He* denoted by the definite article is not identical
with the Logos. The Logos, who is three times in this verse described with the definite article, seems perhaps to stand over against
this He as a second He who is distinct from the first but who
partakes of the same nature and is thus identical in nature. This
would be certain if, as must first be shown, we had the exegetical
right to assume that the Logos is indeed meant to be characterized
as a He by the definite article. I need not say that in this case our
position very definitely points us once again (we have already said
something of the same relative to the *en archē̜ ēn*) in the direction
in which Nicea and the Athanasian Nicenes would later go with
their doctrine of the homoousion, of the essential unity of the different persons or hypostases of the Father and the Son. But if this
is so, then the idea of a so-called reduced deity of the Logos, which
according to Theodor Zahn is possible on the basis of this verse
and is only excluded by v. 2, is already ruled out completely by
v. 1. The thought reached with the third sentence in v. 1 is that the
Logos can belong to God and can be in the beginning with God,
not because he is the person who has the required nature, essence,
or operation in the first instance, or, as we should say in the language of dogmatics, is in the mode of the eternal Father, but because he is the second person, who, as we should say, in the mode
of the eternal Son shares the same nature with the person of the
Father in the same dignity and perfection. One must admit that the
verse makes sense when it is read thus, with the eyes of what has
been called orthodoxy since Nicea. Every word in it is then intelligible in its own place.

    We have inquired into the meaning of the three sentences of
v. 1 without thus far showing any concern for the term around
which they all revolve as around a common axis, the term *ho logos*.
We have acted rightly to the degree that we have simply been study-
ing the emphasis of the three sentences and have seen that in none

of them does it fall on *ho logos*. We have also acted rightly to the
degree that this concept (as a preliminary survey shows), although
it is the subject of the three sentences of v. 1 which are so packed
with content, obviously plays for the author the role of a locum
tenens. It is simply the provisional designation of a place which
something or someone else will later fill. That this apparently chief
concept has the character of a quid pro quo will emerge, as we
must show, from a correct exposition of v. 2. And it will be unequivocally plain at the very latest by the end of the prologue. In
the prologue itself the term will recur only once, although then in
the important statement in v. 14. Later, in the rest of the Gospel,
it will never even be thought of explicitly. And in the rest of the
New Testament there is only one place where it occurs unambig-
uously in the absolute use of John 1:1, namely, in the difficult verse
Rev. 19:13, where it is said of the rider on the white horse that one
of the diadems on his head bears his name, the name that no one
knows (i.e., understands) except himself, and that this name, which
all may read but only he can understand, this ideogram that he
alone can solve, is *ho logos tou theou*. Here again the term holds
a place representatively and in temporary concealment for another
term, the true one, which the white rider himself knows, which
consists of his very existence, as it were, and comes to expression
in it. In the Gospel this relation is very clear. Already in the prologue *ho logos* is a substitute for Jesus Christ. His is the place
which at one and the same time is occupied, reserved, and delimited
by the predicates which are ascribed to the Logos, by the history
which is narrated about him.

But whence and why and in what sense is the term Logos
brought in for this purpose? This is the question that we must now
answer. It is as well to realize that in asking about the whence and
why and in what sense we have two different and not necessarily
related questions. Historically and genetically, in asking whence
the Logos is the subject of these preparatory statements, we are
obviously saying that in using the concept the Evangelist, whether
with or without outside stimulation, is borrowing a well-known
term current in the popular philosophical and religious vocabulary
of his day. That he took it from Philo has for a long time been for
modern expositors a formula that supposedly meets all the facts.
In opposition to this view both more conservative and more critical
research has maintained and admittedly shown that John's concept

of the Logos is in important ways very different from Philo's and certainly must be traced back to other sources. Again in opposition to this objection F. Overbeck (pp. 368ff.) has laid his finger on the point that Philo and John are very different writers, the one a philosopher, the other an Evangelist, so that the latter might well have adopted the Logos concept of the former and then, unconcerned about the special problems and systematizings of the former, freely used it in his own unphilosophical way and for his own purposes. Finally, investigations that are oriented to the history of religion have gone beyond the whole controversy by noting the role that the concept plays not only in Philo and the earlier and later philosophers of antiquity but also in the piety of the mysteries and in the popular religions of Hellenism. They have pointed out that in the age of Hellenism the name and functions of the Logos were assigned to the Greek Hermes, the Egyptian Thoth, and finally the Zoroastrian and Mandean deities of a personal, semi-personal, or impersonal character, the Mandean deities having been more closely examined only within the last decade. In answering the genetic question we thus face a whole ocean of possibilities within which it is a waste of time to seek the lost drop, i.e., the true source of John. First, we do not know at all in what specific form the Evangelist took over the concept, and second, we do not know to what reconstruction he subjected it when he did adopt it. How then can we know the decisive thing, namely, which of the various concepts he adopted? Especially as we do not know for certain that he did in fact "adopt" his concept, i.e., that he received a push in its direction from outside. Let us be content to assert that this at any rate is far more probable than the assumption that Theodor Zahn is making, if I understand him aright, namely, that with no such push from outside, with no reference to the ambivalent commonplace of his day, the Evangelist was led to the concept by inner necessity.

A more important and productive question is that of the meaning of the concept. In answering this question, of course, we turn, not to Philo or the Mandeans, but exclusively to John himself. That is to say, we rule out intrinsically possible meanings whereby the Logos is essentially and primarily a principle, whether in epistemology or in the metaphysical explanation of the world, e.g., as the supreme idea along the lines of Neoplatonism, as creative and ruling cosmic reason along the lines of Stoicism, or as the power of spirit mediating between God and the material world along the lines of Philo. If Philo in particular was the source of John, then, as Overbeck has shown, John has indeed used this source with a sovereign freedom that renders Philo virtually unrecognizable. The same is true of all the ancient philosophies, worldviews, and religions in which deities as principles of being or knowledge, as cosmic principles, are given the name *logos* or *logoi.* For there can be no doubt, as we see unmistakably from the cosmogonic role that is ascribed to the Logos in v. 3 and v. 10, that it is not for the sake of its significance in this regard that the Evangelist has taken up the term. Thus v. 3 recalls the mediating role of the Word in creation, but when we read it in the total context of the prologue it is obviously an episode, a subordinate element in the picture, past which the Evangelist strides on rapidly to his true goal, namely, that the Word is the bearer of life, of the life that was light, the light of humanity in the battle that it has constantly fought with darkness, the Word that today has appeared among us in the flesh, and as *monogenēs,* as *theos,* revealed to us the unknown God. No matter where the writer found his catchword, which is perhaps more than a catchword, this is the Johannine Logos: the Logos as the principle of revelation, not of being, as that which challenges all that is and all being by[17] the divine address that is directed to humanity from person to person. Looking back at the genetic question, we are forced to say that if in relation to the use that John makes of the Logos concept we have to consider some stimulation from outside, then much more likely possibilities than Philo's Logos are the Hellenistic concept of the *hieros logos,* i.e., of sacred and mysterious revelation in the cultus (W. Bauer, op. cit., 8), the Mandean deities, which primarily and essentially are bearers of revelation and are sometimes called "word," and the Hermes and Thoth speculations and myths of the Greeks and Egyptians. But be that as it may, when we ask *why* John used the concept *ho logos* and not, e.g., the *sophia* of later Jewish speculation, we need not fail to answer. It was certainly not because, as W. Bauer (op. cit., 7) thinks, he wanted to equate the preexistent being about whom he planned to speak with a male person, and hence could not use *sophia.* Instead, it was because his interest focused on Jesus Christ, the content of his Gospel, for whom in this mysterious provisional way

---

[17]A: "in virtue of its origin by."

he substitutes this concept in the prologue, and who is for him the Revealer (and strictly only the Revealer according to Bultmann's view). Everything else pales beside the fact that in him God is in the broadest sense speech, address, the Word that comes to us. In him as the Word is the life that is the light of men, as we read in vv. 4f. It seems to me to be making it all impermissibly pragmatic when Schlatter has it that the Evangelist is referring to the words from the lips of Jesus.[18] For the Evangelist the Word is not just the words that Christ speaks but the Word that he is in his whole manifestation. The fact that he is the Word contains and sums up all that he is. For John, then, all the other things fade away which undoubtedly echo in the Logos concept, and of which we might still catch an echo if we have a taste for speculation. In John Logos means Word, and perhaps we do best not to add to this, not even perhaps to make the addition Creator-Word which recollection of Gen. 1:1 suggests. All the things that with historical justification we might read into *ho logos* in the light of contemporary ideas, all the things that with exegetical justification we might read into it in the light of v. 3 and v. 10, e.g., reason, meaning, principle, power, deed, etc., can only cause confusion. We think of the passage in which Goethe has his Faust ("We learn to value supraterrestrial things, we long for revelation") expound the New Testament precisely at this verse: "It is written: In the beginning was the Word. Here I falter already. Who will help me? I cannot possibly value the word so highly. I have to translate it differently if I am truly to be enlightened by the Spirit." He then considers the renderings "meaning" or "power," but finally: "I suddenly see my way and confidently write: In the beginning was the deed."[19] But immediately after he has confidently written this, the devil appears. It would be better to stay with the fact that John calls the subject of his Gospel, his "hero" in the not wholly apt phrase of W. Bauer, "the Word." The word is the unassuming but incomparably true form in which people simply impart themselves, no more and no less, to others. By the Word God, too, imparts himself to us. Because he is the Word of God, he is not just *a* word but *the* Word, the Word of all words.

---

[18]A. Schlatter, "Das Evangelium nach Johannes," in *Erläuterungen zum Neuen Testament,* vol. 1: *Die Evangelien und die Apostelgeschichte.* 3rd ed. (Stuttgart, 1922), p. 1.

[19]J. W. Goethe, *Faust I.* lines 1216f., 1224-1228, 1236f.

But the *Word*. In the simplicity and strictness, and precisely thus in the fulness of the Word, God reveals himself and has revealed himself. From the very first line John starts out from the fact that the Word is and has been given. This need not be proved. We can count on it with the certainty of an axiom. Hence no stress is laid on the threefold *ho logos* in v. 1. As an ideogram it can stand there like the inscription on the diadem of the white rider of Rev. 19, which can be read but not understood, like the *x* in the equation whose value will appear only when the equation is solved. The prologue first sets out the equation. It gives the unknown factor its place, its relation to the other numbers. What is the place of the Word in the economy of the whole complex of God, the world, humanity, the witnesses, believers? What role does it play? What is its path from him who speaks it to those who hear it? What is, what takes place, where it is spoken and heard? Finally, at the climax, who is the Word? But this brings us to the point where the concept has served its turn, where the reality of Jesus Christ that is concealed in the proclamation of the Evangelist takes its place with power, where the equation is solved: *kai hautē estin ē martyria tou Iōannou*, vv. 19ff. We have in v. 1 the beginning of this presentation. The Word is where God is. Hence it must belong to God and be of the same nature as God. No more and no less than God himself was and is needed if the Word is there, and is and will be spoken. *He* had to speak it. But he *has* spoken it. And he speaks it *again*. To this Word the human word of the Evangelist bears witness.

    2. *Houtos* **ēn en archȩ̄ pros ton theon.** This, I think, is how we should place the emphasis. So far as I can see, this verse receives what might be called perfunctory treatment from almost all expositors. The commentaries tell us that it recapitulates, concentrates, confirms, and repeats v. 1. This obviously means that they can make neither head nor tail of it. They cannot tell us why this recapitulation is needed after three short, clear statements, or what purpose it serves. In fact, nothing beyond v. 1, or especially its second and third statements, seems to be said here, and the only surprise is why the third statement is not confirmed and repeated too. Theodor Zahn, who was struck by this, supposes that with the repetition of the two basic statements, namely, that the Logos was *en archȩ̄* and *pros ton theon*, the final statement, namely, that he was *theos*, is safeguarded against the view (which, according to

Zahn's exposition, is not ruled out) that the Logos, like other divine
hypostases, is a supreme creature. No, v. 2 answers according to
Zahn, *he,* the Logos, was in the beginning with God. But apart
from the dubious nature of the assumption regarding v. 1c, it is
very doubtful whether the author would have offered such a safe-
guard by merely repeating v. 1a and v. 1b, statements which, if I
understand him aright, Zahn thinks we are to elucidate in terms
of v. 1c. Where does it leave us, then, if what is elucidated has to
elucidate that which elucidates it? If we cannot follow Zahn, and
find an answer to the riddle of the verse in the theory of mere
recapitulation, there remains only one possibility which, surprisingly, only Schlatter (p. 2) among all the exegetes known to me
takes into consideration. I have to regard it as the only possibility.
Why should the *houtos ēn* merely refer back to *ho logos?* Can it
not also point forward in some way? Is it arbitrary to hunt around
in the prologue and to argue that another highly significant *houtos
ēn* occurs in v. 15, in the saying of the Baptist, in which *houtos ēn,*
although the name is not mentioned, undoubtedly refers to Jesus?
In the whole development in vv. 1-18 the author obviously has Jesus
Christ in view. He is referring to him. For him Jesus is the Logos,
Jesus is the life, Jesus is the light that shines in the darkness. All
expositors agree on this. Zahn and Schlatter and also Eduard Thurneysen[20] have all emphasized this very strongly in their interpretations, even too strongly in my view (esp. Zahn with his too great
historicizing). Fundamentally this view of the prologue is unquestionably correct. But it rests primarily on a hypothesis that arises
irresistibly out of the total impression made by the section. Exegetically its correctness can be demonstrated only if the *houtos* of
v. 2 does not refer back to the *ho logos* of v. 1c but is a first and
purely indicatory filling of the place that is marked out by the term
Logos and its predicates in v. 1. After the first and basic statements
that define the place, John, on this view, is saying that he, this one,
who in truth as little needs to be made known as a person as does
the person that we here call *ho theos* — this one whom we all know,
who has come to us all as the Word, who addresses himself to us

---

[20]E. Thurneysen, "Der Prolog zum Johannesevangelium," *Zwischen den
Zeiten.* 3 (1925), 12-37, esp. p. 24; repr. in *Das Wort Gottes und die Kirche.
Aufsätze und Vorträge.* Theologische Bücherei (Munich, 1971), pp. 185-211, esp.
p. 198.

all (the Evangelist immediately adopts here the attitude of John the Baptist with his pointing finger) — he was in the beginning with God, and all that has been said and is yet to be said is said about him. The author can thus rely axiomatically on the fact that the Word has been given and spoken because he is at once in a position to give the indication: *houtos*, "he there," as Schlatter paraphrases the term. With his statement that the Word was in the beginning John looked back to the beginning of the Bible, to creation. But now he speaks about the Word that lends nature its law and its power. "He looks from the beginning of the Bible over to Jesus, and with this first statement he says how thankful he is to Jesus. In him he has so found the Word of God that he can receive it." In my view, this is saying too much, but materially it catches excellently the meaning of the verse. I need not stress the point that the verse, interpreted thus, is no longer superfluous as in earlier expositions. One has to read it in very close connection with v. 1c. With a *backward* reference the meaning is that he, Jesus, as the Logos who was *theos,* who partook of the divine nature, was in the beginning, because as such he belongs legitimately to God. Hence the concrete pointing to Jesus with the remarkable discretion that is proper to the author tells us both who was in the beginning with God, because he was *theos,* and that his being *theos,* his being in the beginning with God, is true. The answer to both questions is that it was *he.* If we view v. 2 in this way, we need not be surprised that the statement in v. 1c is not repeated, for v. 2 is related to it. We are then forced exegetically to understand the *theos ēn ho logos* of v. 1c, as we have done, as an identification by nature of two distinct persons. For alongside the person denoted by *ho theos* the *houtos* that partakes of the same *theotēs,* the Logos, has also come in *person.*

   3. If vv. 1-2 undoubtedly form a first closed circle in the presentation, the same applies to v. 3: **panta di' autou egeneto kai chōris autou egeneto oude hen ho gegonen.** I thus accept this demarcation of the verse. It is debated whether there should not be a period after *oude hen.* If so, *ho gegonen* goes with what follows. W. Bauer (op. cit., p. 11) offers four arguments that seem to favor this reading. (1) The rhythm comes out better (as Loisy points out). (2) There are other instances of what might seem to be the strange ending of the sentence with *oude hen* (as Eduard Schwartz and Bauer himself argue). (3) Citations of the verse in patristic and heretical writings

from the second to the middle of the fourth century predominantly
give it in this form, as Zahn (pp. 708ff.) shows. (4) One suspects
that putting *ho gegonen* at the end of this verse was a measure
taken in the struggle against Arian and Macedonian exegesis. Against
ending the sentence at *oude hen,* however, is the linguistic difficulty
of the expression *ho gegonen . . . zōē ēn,* which one then has to
swallow in v. 4 whether or not one puts a comma after *autō,* and
which very early witnesses try to avoid by substituting *estin* for
the awkward *ēn,* just as *ouden* often replaces *oude hen,* which is
certainly surprising at the end of a sentence. Zahn (p. 52) finds in
this variant reading a reason to reject the ending with *oude hen* in
spite of everything that seems to support it. W. Bauer, after firmly
deciding against this ending in Hand-Commentar (p. 34),[21] comes
out for textual corruption in Handbuch (p. 11). The question stands
indeed on a razor's edge. If I decide with Zahn for ending v. 3 with
ho gegonen, I do so (not without awareness of the great weight of
external arguments against it) for the internal reason that the ending with *oude hen,* i.e., the meaning that it gives to v. 4, namely,
that what came into being was or is life in the Logos — in other
words, cosmogonic speculation in natural philosophy (which is not
present in v. 3 except as a possible deduction in the margin) — then
acquires a breadth and significance and orientation which it cannot
possibly have according to the whole approach of the rest of the
prologue and the Gospel. Just consider what would be the com-
plexion of vv. 4b-5 if the light to which they refer were equated
with the life that for its part is unequivocally equated with everything created! What was created was or is life, and this life is the
light of men! What would such equations mean? If we cannot think
that the author indulged in such speculations — as the church fathers seem to have done — if we try definitely to derive the meaning
of life in v. 4a from the fact[22] that in v. 4b the light of men is
named, with a reference to history and not to nature, if we are right
to regard v. 3, and later v. 10, as an indispensable link, but only a
link, an episode, in the whole train of thought, then, without ruling
out the possibility of textual corruption, we shall believe that, even
apart from linguistic arguments, to begin v. 4 with *ho gegonen* is
not original but an ancient misunderstanding.

---

[21]Cf. n. 14.
[22]A adds: " — we follow a sound instinct if we do — ."

If, although not without some remaining uncertainty, we conclude v. 3 with *ho gegonen*, then both positively and negatively (cf. 1 John 5:12) the verse actually ascribes to the Logos what Philo ascribes to it as an essential function, what is also ascribed to Logos Hermes, to Logos Thoth, to the *sophia* of Prov. 8:30, to Athena and Isis, to Vohu Manah and Mithra in the Zoroastrian religion, and finally to the Mandean Hibil-Ziwa. By it, making use of it, working through it as a representative, God made the world. As we read later in v. 10: *ho kosmos di' autou egeneto.* As we read in 1 Cor. 8:6: *di' hou ta panta.* As we read in Col. 1:16a: *en autō ektisthē ta panta,* and in 16d: *ta panta di' autou . . . ektistai.* As we read finally in Heb. 1:2: *di' hou kai epoiēsen tous aiōnas.* The *dia* in all these passages denotes the role of the means or, rather, of the mediator whose existence and function, in the mind of the author and of that insightful age, explain the unheard-of fact that the dark, lower world is possible and actual alongside the pure and lofty God. Through him and only through him, through the Revealer, is this possible. Natural and revealed theology do not disagree but agree on this point. So great is God that it is only the Revealer who can originally bind him and the world together. So great is the riddle of the world that only the Revealer can secure its original relation to God. So great is the Revealer that in him we see not merely a later, ad hoc fellowship between God and the world, set up merely for the purpose of redemption, but a fellowship that is original. There would be no point in trying to contest the fact that in thus connecting the Revealer and the Creator, the Evangelist and the other New Testament writers entertain a thought that is not, it would seem, uncommon in their day. We do not reduce the value or significance of the New Testament witness if we acknowledge with some astonishment that many of its most important statements may be heard everywhere in a more or less clear form, that the time (which is said to be "fulfilled" [Gal. 4:4]) seemed to have a general awareness of what needed simply to be given its proper name and proclaimed as a reality by the Christian church. By way of distinction, however, we need to say, of course, that the New Testament authors are not primarily interested in this thought, as to a large extent non-Christian parallels seem to be, for the sake of giving an answer to the riddle of the world. Nor are they primarily interested in it in order to develop some prior doctrine of God. Their primary interest is that in this thought they found, in relation to God and the world, the word which they needed to bring into focus the reality of the Revealer as they believed they knew it in[23] Jesus Christ. Jesus Christ was their first concern, God and the world their second concern. I am not in a position to decide whether one can speak about a similar relation between God, the world, and the Revealer in any of the other speculations about the mediator. This is the relation, however, in the New Testament. The aim is to give Jesus Christ his place, and then to give God and the world their places. What Calvin rightly says about this verse applies to the other New Testament passages as well: *haec practica est notitia.*[24]

So much regarding the general meaning of the verse. Compared to the other New Testament passages mentioned it has three special nuances. First, it does not use *ta panta* but *panta* without the article. As a glance at passages like Rom. 8:28 and 1 Cor. 3:21 teaches us, and as the *oude hen* of the verse itself confirms, this means that the author is not looking at the world as a whole but at the world as the sum total of its individual parts. His point is that everything that has come into being, absolutely all things without exception, has come into being through the Logos. Again, he does not say that they were created, or that God created them, but *egeneto,* "they came into being." The emergence of things is not seen from above but from below, in terms of themselves, as their own function. Yet this very quality of what they themselves do, their coming into being, is relativized. It is not their own. They have come into being not through themselves but through the Logos. Finally, the second and negative part of the saying underlines and sharpens it in a way that does not happen in the other New Testament sayings. Nothing, not one single thing, *ne unum quidem,* none of the many things that are (as the perfect *gegonen* is to be understood) came into being without the Logos, independently of him, or apart from him.

Supported by the establishment of these nuances, we ob-

---

[23]A: "not in Thoth or in Hermes or in Hibil-Ziwa, but in."

[24]See Calvin's *Commentarius in Evangelium Ioannis,* Corpus Reformatorum LXXV, col. 4. [Cf. the English translation by T. H. L. Parker, *The Gospel according to St. John, 1-10.* Calvin's New Testament Commentaries, vol. 4, ed. D. W. Torrance and T. F. Torrance (repr. Grand Rapids, 1979), p. 9: "It is in this practical knowledge that we ought especially to be trained."]

viously cannot be content with what we have said generally by way
of understanding the thought. We must go on to ask in what further
sense the Evangelist believed he had to say precisely this at this
point. We might find many more or less true things stated in the
verse. Thus Augustine[25] took occasion to warn his listeners against
the Manichean doctrine of an independent origin of evil, which
seems tempting in view of the existences of flies and fleas. No, he
cries, all things from angels to worms were created by the Word.
We suffer evil, among other things from such insects, because we
have offended God. According to Pfleiderer and Grill[26] the Evangelist finds himself here in conflict with the Gnostic doctrine of
aeons and archons. Of all such interpretations one might say that
although the verse might have such meanings they are strangely
remote from the context. Schlatter's exposition is that with the
Word that was with God we are given all that we need in relation
to the world, for the Word is the power that made the world.[27] The
passage does contain this thought too, but it does not bring us any
closer to its specific meaning. Nearer to the actual statement is the
insight of Calvin that John, having taught the deity of the Word in
vv. 1-2, now wants to show how the Word is at once at work in
and with creation, how, emerging from its inconceivable being in
God, it may be known in its works.[28] Those are all looking in the
same direction who think they see the point of the prologue in the
anticlimax: The Word with God, the Word and the world, the Word
among men, the Word itself flesh. That this anticlimax is present,
and that here we are on the second highest rung of the ladder, we
obviously cannot dispute. I should say that this anticlimax forms
the framework of consideration, and that descending this ladder,
with the valuable insights that it yields, undoubtedly forms the
general purpose of the prologue. What seems to be arguable to me,
however, is that the purpose of the prologue is exhausted by the
descent of this ladder from rung to rung. We recall what we said
about its practical purpose. The nuances that we have established

---

[25]Augustine, *Tractatus* . . . . I, 13-15 (op. cit., pp. 11-14). [Cf. Eng. tr.
pp. 11f.]

[26]Quoted in Holtzmann, op. cit., p. 34.

[27]Cf. A. Schlatter, *Erläuterungen*, op. cit., p. 2: Schlatter has "that made
all things."

[28]J. Calvin, loc. cit. [Cf. Eng. tr. pp. 9f.]

in v. 3 — the sharpening of the thought of *ta panta di' autou* by the
negative repetition, the climax with the individual *panta* and *oude
hen, egeneto* instead of "they were created" — must all be given their
due in our exposition. The obvious conclusion is that the author
finds himself in a defensive posture, not against the idea that some
entities other than the Logos might be the creative world principle,
but against the idea that within the world itself, in the circle of
what is made, there might be some[29] entity whose coming into
being is independent of the Logos, which evolves of itself and is
thus, so to speak, immediate to God. No, he says, nowhere in the
world is there any immediacy to God. Through the Logos not just
some things, or many things, or most things, or almost all things,
but *all* things came into being. He, as the one who was in the
beginning, who did not himself come into being, who has his place
with God and is himself God, stands on the other side of the boundary which is set for all being as such, i.e., for all that has come
into being. How? In such a way that all of which it is said *gegonen*
in no sense stands alongside him or is what it is *chōris autou,*
without him. Everything that has come into being is completely
different from him. Over against him it stands in that total relativity
which can be expressed precisely and radically only by the *di' autou,* by the concept of creation. This is how things are with all that
is. It is related to God. It is something and not nothing. But it is
something only as it is related to the Word. Its existence is con-
ceivable only in the light of the Word. Its own function is lent it by
the Word, by the Word that was *theos.* As I see it, the special point
of the second little circle of the prologue that we find in v. 3 is to
remind us of that boundary within which everything that is in the
world finds itself. It does not have the same direct relationship to
God as the Word does. Its own relationship to God is mediate,
indirect:[30] it depends upon the Word of God. We have to reckon
with this from the very first vis-à-vis every entity in the world. We
have to view and test every entity in this light. We have to appraise
and place every entity accordingly. A criterion is obviously set up
here. Why? To what end? Baldensperger[31] replies: with a view to

---

[29]The typescript has *welche* here, the printed text *irgend eine.*
[30]A: "indirect, broken."
[31]W. Baldensperger. *Der Prolog des 4. Evangeliums. Sein polemisch-
apologetischer Zweck* (Freiburg, 1898), p. 5.

John the Baptist. Thus stated, this sounds rather blunt and improbable on a first hearing. The reference cannot be to John the Baptist alone, as we have seen in our introduction. But the clue that Baldensperger follows is a genuine one. There is a connection between the *egeneto* of v. 3 and that of v. 6. And if we were right to see a reference to Jesus in the *houtos* of v. 2 as well as in v. 15, we are not grossly mistaken to find in v. 3 a real reference to the Baptist and to the witnesses and preachers of the Word. Whoever belongs to the created world has no independent existence or function over against him who is called *houtos* in v. 2. All of them have their existence and function only *di' autou*, or, as we might meaningfully continue with the parallel Col. 1:16, which speaks similarly of angelic powers, *eis auton*. The witness is not the Revealer, nor is he a witness to himself but to the Revealer. To be sure, this is not yet said in v. 3, but within the total context the way is undoubtedly prepared for it. And in this preparatory purpose I discern the special Johannine emphasis with which the contemporary idea of the mediating role of the Logos is adopted, the concern which causes the author to pause for a moment on this rung of the anticlimax.

4. **En autǭ zōē ēn kai hē zōē ēn to phōs tōn anthrōpōn.** The first point to strike us grammatically is the shift from *zōē* to *hē zōē*. One is tempted to see a similar relation to that between *theos* and *ho theos* in v. 1, and thus to treat *zōē* as an impersonal quality that the Logos shares and *hē zōē* as the same quality personified. But this would not lead anywhere. For in this case the Gnostics would be right to find the aeon *hē zōē* taught here. When Jesus calls himself *hē zōē* in 11:25 and 14:6, this shows that *hē zōē* is no more itself a person than is *zōē*. It is a quality, a value, that finds personified manifestation in a real person, namely, in this person, and that can thus be ascribed to this person. This does not take place in the present verse. Like the personification "I am the light" (8:12; 9:5), it is known, confessed, and presupposed, but it is not yet made. We do not read here *autos* but *en autǭ zōē ēn;* and of this life that is enclosed and contained by the Logos, and that thus characterizes the Logos, the second half of the statement speaks. The material point of the first half comes out in 5:26, which says that as the Father has life (*zōē* without the article) in himself, so he has given it to the Son to have life in himself. And now the second half says that *this* life was the light of men. Hence the relation between *zōē* and *hē zōē* is not the same as that between

theos and *ho theos* in v. 1, but the same as that between *thronos* and *ton thronon* in Rev. 4:2. The definite article has demonstrative significance. This life that dwells in the Logos, characterizes it, and is given to it, was as such, as *hē en autǭ zōē*, the light of men. Historically and genetically it may be noted that John's vocabulary or conceptual material is in no way original. In the Hellenistic world *phōs* is often the proper name of Soter, the saving deity, or even of primal man (thought of as deliverer). The two words *zōē* and *phōs* are often combined in the same way. Thus Poimandres unites them as the two things that denote the origin of humanity and the goal that is to be reached by cleansing. In Mandean works we find the same dependence of light on life as here; we read of the light that rests on the mouth of the first life, or of the light that was from life, with reversals of the relationship as well. God as well as life, e.g., Serapis,[32] is also called the "light of men" in the same phrase as that of the present verse. Undoubtedly, then, there are links with religious history, and I can appeal to the plain content of the verse itself, especially the second half, when I say that all this is correct. It seems to me to be hardly fair that the readers of such a wide-ranging commentary as that of Zahn hear nothing at all about such things. Yet these connections tell us nothing about the meaning that the terms *zōē* and *phōs* have here. We shall see later, however, that it is by no means a waste of time to take note of them.

Let us begin by considering that a new and third train of thought, which is concluded in v. 5, begins in v. 4. The life that was in the Logos is the light of man, and it shines in the darkness, but the darkness does not cease to be darkness. This is the point. By life, provisionally and very generally, redemption is meant, and by light revelation. But we shall have to prove the correctness of our interpretation against a whole flock of exegetes, many of whom have to be taken very seriously. According to H. J. Holtzmann (Hand-Commentar, pp. 34f.) v. 4 is the answer to a question supposedly implied in v. 3: How can all things have come into being

---

[32]Cf. W. Bauer, op. cit., pp. 12f.; W. Bousset, *Kyrios Christos. Geschichte des Christusglaubens von den Anfängen des Christentums bis Irenäus.* 2nd ed. (Göttingen, 1921), pp. 174f. [See the English translation by J. E. Steely, *Kyrios Christos: A History of the Belief in Christ from the Beginnings of Christianity to Irenaeus* (Nashville, 1970), pp. 233ff.]

from the Logos, how can there have been a principle of creation?
The answer is: Because according to his depicted relation to God
his content was life, a being that brings forth other being. Thus
exposition of v. 4b has to run as follows: The power of life that
streams forth from him proves especially to be a means of illumination vis-à-vis the human world. Many have previously followed
this track, seeing in *zōē* the general life of creation (with a reference
back to v. 3), and in *hē zōē* the life that illumines humanity. "Le
Logos était [comme dit Schaff] la vie de chaque vie."[33] Thus Augustine understands by "life" the existence of all things in the ideas,
or in *the* idea, insofar as they have true existence in the idea. Apart
from the idea they are bodies; in the idea, *en autō*, they are life.
But human beings are rational souls as they perceive the idea, i.e.,
as they receive the Word, as they are illumined by this true life of
things.[34] "*Augustinus more suo nimium platonicus ad ideas rapi-
tur,*" comments Calvin, and he finds the thought of the church
father "*a mente evangelistae longe remotum.*" [See Eng. tr. p. 10:
"Augustine, who is in his way an extreme Platonist, is addicted to
the concept of the idea, . . . far . . . from the thought of the Evangelist."] But Calvin's own exposition, which does not platonize, or
perhaps platonizes in its own way, moves remarkably along the
very same lines. Calvin finds in *zōē* the *continua inspiratio* that
takes place by the Word. By this means God, having made the
world, constantly sustains it. In *hē zōē*, however, Calvin finds the
life of the spirit which distinguishes humanity from the beasts. In
this — undoubtedly a deeper and truer thought — the Word of God
that is the basis of all things is reflected as in a mirror.[35] Also along
the same lines, but more crudely in the spirit of the nineteenth
century, A. Tholuck explains that God as the self-revealing God is
the source of natural life; in humanity this natural life appears at
its highest potency as consciousness, as direct perception.[36] Meyer,
too, writes that the reference is to the general life source of the

---

[33]F. Godet, *Commentaire sur l'Evangile de Saint Jean,* II (Paris/Neuchâtel,
1885), p. 49. [Eng. tr. *Commentary on John's Gospel,* tr. T. Dwight (repr. Grand
Rapids, 1978), p. 252: "The Logos was, as *Schaff* says, 'the life of every life.' "]
[34]Augustine, op. cit., I, 17 (pp. 15f.). [See Eng. tr. p. 12.]
[35]J. Calvin, op. cit., col. 47. [See Eng. tr. p. 11.]
[36]A. Tholuck, *Commentar zu dem Evangelio Johannis,* 2nd ed. (Hamburg,
1828), p. 43.

world that was made by the Logos, who as such could not be
inactive, at least in relation to humanity, but who necessarily had
to show himself to be at work in it according to its rational nature.[37]
In a sermon on this text Schleiermacher used the same thought to
make the point that the individual human soul does not see only
what is dead around it but also sees life, which leads it to a knowledge of God as the author of the world, so that earthly life, the life
that encounters us in the world, is in fact the light of men.[38] And
finally, again in a sermon, and within the framework of this view
coming closest to the truth, Luther distinctively claims that "natural
life is a part of eternal life and only a beginning, but it comes to an
end through death, because it does not recognize him from whom
it comes; the same sin cuts it off, so that it has to die eternally.
Again, those who believe and recognize him from whom they have
life never die, but natural life is strengthened to eternal life, so that
it never tastes of death."[39]

I cannot deny that the presupposition underlying this whole
understanding, namely, that v. 4a is looking back to v. 3, is not in
itself improbable. At v. 3 we recalled the parallels in Col. 1:16 and
Heb. 1:2, and it might well be pointed out that in those passages
we go on to read: *ta panta en autǭ synestēken* (Col. 1:17), and:
pherōn te ta panta tǭ rhēmati tēs dynameōs autou (Heb. 1:3), to
which the *en autǭ zōē ēn* of this verse aptly corresponds according
to that understanding, especially in Calvin's formula: *"continua
inspiratio mundum vegetans."* But we can obviously presuppose
such a reference back to v. 3 — and this is the second presupposition
of that understanding — only if the decisive concept *zōē* permits

---

[37]H. A. W. Meyer. *Kritisch exegetisches Handbuch über das Evangelium
des Johannes*, 4th ed. (Göttingen, 1862). p. 57. [See the English translation by
W. Urwick. *A Critical and Exegetical Hand-book to the Gospel of John*. rev. and
ed. F. Crombie (New York, 1895). pp. 50f.]

[38]F. Schleiermacher, *Homilien über das Evangelium des Johannes, in den
Jahren 1823 und 1824 gesprochen*. vol. I (Berlin, 1837), p. 10.

[39]M. Luther. *Evangelium in der hohen Christmesse. Johannes 1:1-14* (Kir-
chenpostille 1522), WA 10, I, p. 200. Barth deviates from the text by putting an
"only" before "beginning," and he follows C. G. Eberle, *Luthers Evangelien-
Auslegung. Ein Kommentar zu den vier Evangelien*, 2nd ed. (Stuttgart, 1877), by
putting "strengthened" for "lengthened" in the second sentence. [Cf. the English
translation by M. H. Bertram. *Sermons on the Gospel of St. John. Chapters 1-4*.
Luther's Works, vol. 22. ed. J. Pelikan (St. Louis, 1957), p. 29.]

and commands it. And this, it would seem to me, is not the case in that I know of no passage in the whole of John's Gospel where it is possible to equate *zōē* with being that brings forth other being, with the life of all things in the idea, with *continua inspiratio*. with the source of life, etc. Always in this Gospel the term *zōē* (with or without the addition *aiōnios*) has soteriological-eschatological significance. It is the life which, as we have already affirmed in the light of 5:26, the Son has in himself (*en heautǭ*) as the Father has given him to do so. In contrast to *apōleia* and *thanatos* it is the imperishable being, not subject to corruption or destruction, which through the Revealer, as the decisive thing that he has to bring according to John, is offered to all people and imparted to those who believe in him, through him who at some climaxes is himself called *hē zōē*. This and not anything else is what *zōē* means in 6:33 and 6:51, where we read of *zōē kosmou*. In these passages the *kosmos* is unquestionably the human world and *zōē* is none other than the life that is imparted to this world by the Revealer. *Zōē* in John's Gospel is not the life that is already in us or the world by creation; it is the new and supernatural life which comes in redemption and has first to be imparted to us in some way. Is it really permissible to assume that precisely here we have an exception and that what is meant is the natural life that is lent by God to all creatures as such? Is it not more likely that precisely at this point where it occurs for the first time it has to be used in the pregnant sense that it bears in the rest of the Gospel?

Coming now to the third presupposition of that understanding, we find that things are the same with the subordinate concept of *phōs*. I have still to find in John a passage in which light is the light which is present by creation, which is given in and with the life of creation, which is there as the uncreated light of the created world, which does not rather come only with the life of redemption, which is not the light of revelation. which perhaps comes from the very beginning but still comes. In relation to v. 3 we referred to the coincidence of revealed theology and natural theology both there and in the New Testament parallels. But it seems to me to be characteristic of New Testament thinking—I make the same point regarding the well-known verse Rom. 1:19—that with a strict reserve appropriate to the theme it does not use the insight that the Revealer is also the Creator in such a way that by a logical inversion (all things are possible in logic!) it is also said that the Creator is

the Revealer. God's self-revealing is a separate action that goes
beyond creation. In relation to what was made, to its life and to
the knowledge that may be gained from it, *phōs* is a new and
different light which is only arising. It is the light of dawn, not the
full light of eternity already present.[40] Note that the apparently
very tempting *hē zōē ēn to phōs* of this verse is given in v. 9 the
interpretation: *ēn to phōs erchomenon eis ton kosmon.* This seems
to me to oppose sharply that understanding, in spite of the vener-
able names associated with it, since it does not do justice to the
strict character of revelation as *phōs erchomenon.* And finally, in
view of our initial grammatical findings, we have to ask its champions what they make of the change from *zōē* to *hē zōē,* in which
we can find the distinction between the life of creation and the life
of the human spirit only by violent wresting. If this counterargu-
ment is cogent, as I believe, then in v. 4a we are not to look back.
We have to consider a new thought — in brief the whole complex of
reconciliation[41] and revelation. The religious parallels mentioned
also point us in this direction. After the author has said in v. 3 that
without exception everything made is mediate to God because it is
made by the Word, and that nothing is *chōris autou,* that nothing
has its origin from God directly and apart from the Word, now,
making a new beginning, he goes on to say that in him was life,
namely, the life which is indispensable to men but which in a fearful
way they do not have, the true, authentic, eternal life which is
immune to corruption and death, life such as God has in himself.
That we do not actually have this indispensable thing is stated
indirectly in v. 5, but the reason why this is so is not yet given. We
are undoubtedly right to assume that with the mere mention of the
thoroughly soteriological term *zōē,* implicitly its negative presupposition too (indicated by the *ou katelaben* of v. 5) would be more
than clearly stated for the author's contemporaries. This life, i.e.,
the life that overcomes death, *was* in him.[42] In view of the contin-

---

[40]Cf. the hymn "Morgenglanz der Ewigkeit" by C. A. P. Knorr von Rosenroth.

[41]A: "redemption."

[42]A: "implicitly its negative hamartiological and thanatological presuppositions would be more than clearly stated. It is because sin is in them, and therefore death reigns over them, that men do not have that which is indispensable.
Therefore this life, i.e., salvation, deliverance, victory over sin and death, *was* in
him."

uation in v. 4b, i.e., that it was the light of men, and in view of the
ēn erchomenon with which the same thought is taken up in v. 9,
one has to say that this *ēn* has a significance that goes beyond the
eternal *ēn* of v. 1. We do not rule out that meaning, but here *ēn*
also means that it was, not as one created thing is alongside others,
nor in a permanent relation that is contained from the very first in
the concept of God and the world, but in the unique way in which
this life — in the Word which is spoken from eternity into time, and
which may be heard in time with all the seriousness of eternity —
is present as the life that is indispensable but is still missing,
as the true life that overcomes death. *Is.* I say, although not excluding the *was.* The imperfect *ēn* includes a present here, as may
be seen from the *phainei* that follows in the next verse. In translation we can quietly let the past tense stand, however, only so long
as by the past we do not understand a specific time but all past
history. Thus life was presented to the world. It was set before eyes
and ears in such a way that they could not forget it, or overlook it,
or suppress their unavoidable unrest and longing for it, or deny the
appeal that it signified for them. This redemptive life, v. 4b explains, was (*en autǭ.* contained and offered in God's Word) the
"light of men," the light of revelation which illumined them. Objectively and enduringly there stood before them the possibility or
opportunity of knowing it, of knowing about it. Whatever the result
might be (more of this in v. 5), light was nowhere and never absent.
Nowhere and never was there lacking the chance, provided by the
divine action, to think about life, about salvation, about the life
that is lost and yet not lost inasmuch as it was enclosed and pre-
served and offered in the Word and shone as the light of revelation.
By the Word, as Schlatter paraphrases it,[43] God has worked the
miracle that the life that derives from him appeared on earth and
did not remain hidden.

　　If *zōē* is not the life which is from creation but the life which
in reconciliation[44] is in principle future, i.e., which comes to us,
which in contrast to all our past breaks into our present, and if as
the *phōs tōn anthrōpōn* it is not the light of reason and the like but
revelation, i.e., the redemption which visibly tears down the bar-

---

[43]Op. cit., p. 3.
[44]A: "redemption."

riers of death, we have still to answer the question what specifically the Evangelist has in mind when he speaks these words. If in the exposition thus far I have mostly agreed with Zahn over against the other exegetes, in this question I have to part company with him. Far too one-sidedly and violently, as it seems to me, he rushes on to the interpretation that the reference here is to the "historical person of Jesus." In him was life as distinct from all others, in whom it was not present. In his self-attestation by word and work the life shone for all. This is how he would interpret the verse. Similarly he relates the whole prologue directly and exclusively to the thirty years of the epiphany of the Logos in Jesus of Nazareth.[45] I admit to the suspicion that the principle of orthodox Lutheran christology, *ubicunque est logos, ibi etiam praesentissimam sibi habet carnam,*[46] might have had something to do with Zahn's zeal in this regard. But be that as it may, his view of the matter is one-sided and violent because even he, in vv. 1-3, cannot deny that we have to do with a reality and activity of the Logos that is only pointing ahead to the historical Jesus, and because it is hard to see why the statement which begins there, and which does not start at the Incarnation but simply hastens toward it, preparing the ground for a consideration of the incarnate Word, should suddenly break off here and become what in this case must be called a puzzlingly abstract reference to the significance of the life of Jesus. Certainly we have to say that in every word that John writes he has in view Jesus of Nazareth as the reality that fills out his depiction of the function of the Logos, as the goal toward which he is moving in this remarkable anticlimax. Certainly, if our interpretation of v. 2 is correct, John has been referring in a significant way to Jesus from the very first: *He* was in the beginning with God. Certainly vv. 4-5 are speaking of the same light as that whose epiphany or arising is depicted in vv. 14ff. and which then becomes the theme of the Gospel proper. Every word of the prologue can (and even must) be related to Jesus of Nazareth, for every word is thought out in re-

---

[45]Zahn, op. cit., p. 45.

[46]H. Schmid, *Die Dogmatik der evangelisch-lutherischen Kirche, darge-stellt und aus den Quellen belegt.* 4th ed. (Frankfurt/Erlangen, 1858), p. 230, quoting J. Gerhard, *Loci theologici* (1657), Locus Quartus, n. 121, tomus I (Leipzig, 1885, p. 502). [See Eng. tr., *The Doctrinal Theology of the Evangelical Lutheran Church* (Philadelphia, 1899), p. 308.]

lation to him, i.e., to the revelation that took place in him.[47] Yet the word "light" includes not only the sunrise but also the dawn when the sun has not yet risen, and even the half-light of the night. It does not seem to me to be the presupposition of the prologue that the existence of light in the world, its coming into the world, to which v. 9 and then 3:19 and 12:46 refer, begins only with the *ensarkōsis* of v. 14. *"Lux luxit etiam antequam in carne appareret."*[48] Inasmuch as every word here relates to Jesus Christ, it also relates to the Logos as the Revealer of God who announces himself before and even apart from Jesus of Nazareth. To the conjectured dogmatic background of Zahn's view we might reply with a principle of orthodox Reformed christology: *"Sic logos naturam humanam sibi univit, ut totus eam inhabitet et tote quippus immensus et infinitus extra eam sit."*[49] I shall be careful not to advance in relation to v. 4 the counterthesis that the reference here is simply to a pre-Christian stage of revelation, e.g., to Israel. The notes sounded by the terms "life" and "light" are too full to permit this. Obviously no one time is here marked off from another. Revelation as a whole, the light which comes and has already come, the light which is the light of men, is here contrasted with history as a whole. What the author wants to say is that whatever was revelation, the light of life, redemption for men, was so only in him — again not directly or immediately from God, from God indeed, but in him, in the same Word that took flesh in Jesus Christ, alongside which there never has been or can be any other Word. In *him* was life, and *this* life was the light of men. The emphasis of the verse — we must not let this be lost — is on the *en autǭ*. Wherever there was light, it was this light. Apart from him there is only witness to the light (v. 8), just as outside him nothing came into being that is. Augustine, even though in the main point he is wrong about this verse as *"nimium platonicus,"* is right, and grasps the thought of

---

[47]A: "i.e., to the revelation which was effected and, as it were, broke through in him."

[48]J. Cocceius, *Evangelium secundum Ioannem cum commentario* (Lugduni Batavorum, 1620), p. 9.

[49]H. Heppe, *Die Dogmatik der evangelisch-reformierten Kirche. dargestellt und aus den Quellen belegt* (Elberfeld, 1861), p. 305, quoting S. Maresius, *Collegium theologicum.* 6th ed. (Geneva, 1662), IX, 30 (p. 118). [Cf. the Eng. tr. of Heppe by G. T. Thomson, *Reformed Dogmatics* (repr. Grand Rapids, 1978), p. 418.]

the Evangelist very well, when he comments on the phrase *to phōs tōn anthrōpon*: "John the Baptist was illumined by this light, and so was John the Evangelist himself. He was full of this light who said: 'I am not the Christ, but he who comes after me.' . . . He was illumined by this light who said: 'In the beginning was the Word, and the Word was with God, and God was the Word.' "[50] Here we take our red thread[51] in our hands again. It is as well not to miss here, too, the accompanying note of this problem.

5. **Kai to phōs en tḗ skotia̧ phainei, kai hē skotia auto ou katelaben.** The readoption of the term *phōs* from v. 4b (which gives significance to the first connecting *kai*), the fact that v. 5a is in some sense an explanation of v. 4b, since it was as the light shining in the darkness that the life was the light of men, these factors justify our assumption that v. 5 stands in a special relation to v. 4 in the same way as v. 2 does to v. 1. The change from *ēn* to *phainei*, which is surprising at first glance, is no argument against this. We have already seen from v. 3b how flexible the tenses are for the author. We shall find further examples in the prologue when we come to v. 9 and v. 15a. As the *ēn* of v. 4 has some present significance, so indubitably the *phainei*, as the contrasting aorist *katelaben* shows, embraces the past as well. In this regard one has to say, of course, that in John the present always has the ring of the special actuality of the event denoted by the verb in question. For the moment I will leave open the question of the special thing at issue and in a preliminary way simply point out that the historical part of the first chapter, the story of Lazarus in ch. 11, and finally the resurrection in chs. 20-21 are all marked by a strikingly fluid use of the present tense which, in places where readers would expect past tenses, necessarily confronts them with the events narrated and hauls them out of their seats to action on the stage. That the surprising *martyrei* of v. 15a of the prologue has this effect is beyond dispute. Is this the aim here too, and also with the *phōtizei* of v. 9? However that may be, the relation in v. 4, which in appearance at least is neutrally described ("The life was the light of men"), is now characterized. It takes on color and becomes dramatic. The presuppositions of the terms "life" and "light," which v. 4 does not specify, now come to the fore. Light shines — this is

---

[50]Op. cit., I, 18 (pp. 16f.). [See Eng. tr. p. 13.]
[51]A: "not from Overbeck, but from Augustine."

an analytical statement — in the darkness. Revelation confronts non-revelation,[52] concealment, indeed, a power that acts inimically against revelation. This is *skotia*. That *skotia* is not identical with the *hoi anthrōpoi* of v. 4 we can see from 3:19, where the men who love the dark, *to skotos*, more than the light are obviously distinguished from darkness. According to the relatively few passages in which *skotia* occurs in John, darkness is the atmosphere which contends against light and redemption. Men, all men, walk in this atmosphere (8:12; 12:35; 1 John 2:11). But as disciples of Jesus they must no longer walk in it; as believers they must not abide in it (12:35, 46). But according to 12:35 darkness can still overtake (*katalambanein*, the same term as in v. 5b) once again those who walk in the light, like a mist that unexpectedly rises in the mountains.

It has often been noted, and quite correctly, that John does not explain why revelation is revelation in the darkness. He has given no origin for this opponent of revelation. He has set it in no relation to the *panta di' autou*, either by explaining that it is an exception, that it has its own genesis, or by explaining that it is included, that evil falls within God's plan for the world. The question of its origin is neither posed nor answered. "The Evangelist has not reflected on it," is the comment of H. Holtzmann[53] on this silence. We must add, however, that this is not because he unfortunately never thought about this profound question. It is because it was for him a meaningless question. *Skotia* is for him a reality which is found on the plane where one cannot put the question of origin, where there is no possibility of objective consideration, where our only option is to reckon with the realities that arise there and to deal with them either in war or in peace. On the same plane there stands on the other side the Word of God in which the self-revealing life is contained. In this case, too, there is no question of origin, of why or whence. In this case, too, there is only the *question de fait*, not *de droit*, for *theos ēn ho logos* (v. 1). Naturally darkness is not for John a second god as it is for Marcion. We are not in fact to restrict the *panta di' autou* (v. 3). At the same time we are not to excuse or explain the fact of darkness with the help of the *panta di' autou*. Incomprehensible in its origin, it confronts the light. It

---

[52]A: "non-revelation, a lack of desire or ability for revelation, for life and redemption."

[53]H. J. Holtzmann, op. cit., p. 37.

LIBRARY, UNIVERSITY OF CHESTER

is not just an isolated phenomenon but the atmosphere, the characteristic constitution of humanity to which revelation turns. It is the dark riddle for the sake of which revelation is necessary and on account of which it can be understood only as a miracle. One might say that we confront the same incomprehensibility in face of darkness and in face of the light that streams from the life of the Word, positive on the one side, negative on the other. The revelation of v. 4 is a new thing compared to v. 3. It is unforeseen. It does not arise out of the plan or reality of creation. If in fact *panta di' autou,* what need is there of the special life that comes, or of its revelation? Revelation has no basis or origin, or it is not revelation. Similarly, the darkness is simply there. It is an incident. It is not part of any program. Opposed to every program, it is simply an event. This incident on the one side and the Word of the revelation of life on the other are what the Evangelist finds to be the determinations of human existence, i.e., of his own existence. Hence he cannot "reflect" on them. Both of them, if in different ways, are incomprehensible. Hence in different ways he can only take up an attitude to both as to facts of an existence that is determined by both. He cannot possibly contemplate them or ask the reasons for them. He can only set them alongside himself. The ugly formula "dualism" does not fit the Johannine antithesis of light and darkness. As the silence shows, there can be no question here of any worldview, of any "ism," of any system. We simply have a conflict in which the Evangelist finds himself engaged and in which — perhaps this explains the urgent *phainei* — he wants to engage his readers. Or rather, he wants to teach his readers that he is engaged in this conflict. He does not philosophize about two world principles. Like a watchman on a tower he signals the approach of armies from the east and from the west. He proclaims imminent decision.

But all this is only incidental and implicit in the verse. The true point of v. 5 is to make a further statement about the role and significance of the Logos. The light shines in the darkness. Its revelation means antithesis, conflict, strife. To be the light of men is to stand against a world of enemies. If we have interpreted v. 4 correctly, and if we are right about the special connection between v. 4 and v. 5, then the only point of v. 5 is to stress the isolation in which the light shines for men, in which the light concealed in the Word manifests itself. As life is in the Word alone, and the life concealed in the Word alone is light, so (v. 5) the light is alone

among men, for men are in darkness. The world and history are
hostile to the light as a whole. It is not at all true that in and from
them there is goodwill, an ability and readiness to receive, that
receptivity corresponds to the light and runs to meet it. Note already here what will be said later in vv. 12-13 about the possibility
of such receptivity. Those who receive him are born of God. Apart
from this possibility what meets the light in men is darkness. Men
are trapped in darkness, in revolt and rejection. A No stubbornly
confronts the Yes. This is the actual situation between the Word
and those to whom it is directed. V. 5b confirms from the other
side, from the human side, that the darkness has not comprehended
the light. It had no power to appropriate it, to make it its own, to
cease to be darkness and itself to become light. This is how we
must translate and understand the statement. The meaning "to
overtake," which *katalambanein* perhaps has in 12:35, is not possible here. The meaning "to restrict," "to overpower," "to conquer,"
which Zahn especially among more recent commentators es-
pouses,[54] seems to be too uncertain and yields a sense which, excellent though it is in itself — the darkness does not master the
light — disrupts the context in most unheard-of fashion. We read in
Rom. 9:30 of a *katalambanein* of righteousness and in 1 Cor. 9:24
and Phil. 3:12 of a *katalambanein* of the heavenly prize, and it is
along these lines that we are to seek the meaning of the striking
term. John is trying to say that the light stands in conflict with an
opponent which by nature could not become its friend even if it
wanted to do so. It is in a conflict that cannot end with a compro-
mise. Darkness has never appropriated the light and never will.
The light, when it shines, can expect nothing from the darkness
except that it was and is and will be darkness. Its conflict can only
be one of decision and destruction. H. Holtzmann and W. Bauer
refer in this regard to a "tragic note," to the "pessimism" of the
passage.[55] This is wrong. We shall see that such terms are out of
place in vv. 10f. too. They certainly do not fit here. What is here
said about the light is in keeping with what was said about it before
(very objectively, without the evaluation or elucidation inherent in
the terms): The Word was God by nature. All things have their

---

[54]T. Zahn, op. cit., p. 36.
[55]H. J. Holtzmann, op. cit., p. 36, speaks of the "tragic note" and W. Bauer,
op. cit., p. 13, of a "tone of pessimism."

origin in him. In him is redemption. This redemption is revelation.
And now, filling out the last point, the statement is made that
revelation takes place in the darkness, that it is isolated, that it
involves a decisive conflict. This is not tragedy. If we are to use an
aesthetic figure, it is an epic. It is a final hymn to the unique dignity
and significance of the Word. This hymn is, of course, austere and
exclusive. It humbles all flesh. Yet it is also bright and proud. It
crowns all that has gone before. In no sense is it pessimistic. This,
I think, is how we are to take the whole passage 1:1-5, which is
now behind us. Perhaps, if we have spoken aright about the rhythm
of the verse, this is also its best explanation from a literary standpoint. Materially I regard it as the only possible one.

6. **Egeneto anthrōpos apestalmenos para theou, onoma autou
Iōannēs.** This verse seems to transport us at a stroke into another
world. Here is the break in the prologue of which we spoke in the
Introduction. I shall not return to that. A literary question perhaps
arises here. In this and the next verses the author has perhaps
worked over a non-Christian original that may go back in some way
to the Mandean world and corrected its statements about John the
Baptist. However that may be, there can be no doubt that he is
speaking about what is for him a pressing issue. We thus have the
right and the duty, in respect of these verses, to relate our own
concern to their form and place in John's Gospel. If they disturb
us — and in some way this reaction is certainly justified — then we
have to ascertain the significance of the disruption which the author
himself effects either with his own or with alien materials. Or
rather, we have to ascertain the sense in which these statements
are obviously intended to alert his readers and suddenly to steer
their thoughts in a new direction.

Our thoughts do in fact have to make a leap from v. 5 to v. 6
after moving step by step, if very vigorously, from v. 1 to v. 5. The
surprising element in v. 6 is that it plunges us into the *inside* of
the history that has as it were been illumined from outside in
vv. 4-5. All at once it leads us factually to a *specific point* in the
history, and not, as the sharp contrast of v. 5 would lead us to
expect, immediately to the epiphany of the Logos, but to one of the
points in the history which according to v. 5 undoubtedly must lie
in the sphere of *skotia.* What is the point? This is the question that
v. 6 obviously poses for us in drastic fashion as we move on from
v. 5. *Egeneto* means "there appeared," "there came," "there once

was," according to Zahn.[56] In any case a historical appearance is at issue, a personal coming, a coming within the world, the appearance of one of those existent things, of one of those factors which according to v. 3 (the use of *egeneto* here and in v. 14 as well as in v. 3 is no accident!) comes under the common denominator of *di' autou*, belonging to the plane of creatureliness or relativity in contrast to the Word. Certainly it is not the Word itself, nor anything equal to it, that appears at this point. The *egeneto* unquestionably declares this. That *egeneto* will also be used of the Word in v. 14 represents a further and steep step on the way which we must not presuppose as already apparent if we are to evaluate the text aright. What we see in v. 6, in the light of what precedes, is the contrast between the Logos and all that has come into being. He to whom v. 6 refers is to be seen on this side of the contrast. The *anthrōpos* confirms this. As distinct from *egeneto*, John never uses it for the Logos, or later in the Gospel for Jesus (or only incidentally in 8:40). As a man the one referred to here is one of those for whom the life contained in the Logos was and is light (v. 4), light that shines in the darkness (v. 5). If the *egeneto* and the *anthrōpos* definitely distinguish him from the Logos, the predicate *apestalmenos para theou* brings him close, and even in a sense puts him in the same sphere and gives him the same function. For the same verb (along with *pempein* elsewhere) describes Jesus also as "sent by God" in 5:36, 38; 7:29; 20:21. In the Mandean literature, too, the Revealer himself is "sent" by the higher deity. But it is more relevant here to think of the Old Testament concept of a "sending" of prophets, servants, and angels — *the* angel of God in Mal. 3:1, 23 [Eng. 4:5]. This last passage played a considerable role in the Christian assessment of John the Baptist. Within the world that has come into being, within the human world that has fallen under darkness, not as an exception to the determinations that are posed for all and every creature, there is among the determinations this qualification: sending by God, separation for a task or mission, and in this sense prophecy. "A man, i.e., one who was not previously anything but an ordinary man, was afterward sent by God," is the correct paraphrase of Schleiermacher.[57] And Calvin makes the essential distinction: *"Angeli magis quam hominis per-*

---

[56]T. Zahn, loc. cit.

[57]F. Schleiermacher, op. cit., p. 17.

sonam sustinet. Non suarum virtutum elogiis ornatur, sed hoc uno, quod Dei legatus fuerit."[58]

Already in the Introduction we have discussed the *onoma autǭ Iōannēs* (3:1 introduces Nicodemus in the same way), the semi-obscurity which in part surrounds this name, and the general nature of the problem that this ambivalence raises. If we take vv. 9ff. into account, if we are right to view vv. 6ff. not as an abruptly interposed fragment but as an introduction to vv. 9ff., then we cannot fail to see that in spite of the concretely historical character of vv. 6ff. the author is unwilling to go on directly to an account of the mission of the Baptist. Even in vv. 14ff., where the Baptist appears again in a new context, and even speaks, this will not happen. It does so only in vv. 19ff. with the true beginning of the Gospel. Are we wrong to think that with a view to vv. 9ff. the Baptist does not represent himself in vv. 6ff. but represents all that comes under the concept of *phōs erchomenon eis ton kosmon,* of light as dawn, advent, approaching Christmas, or, more concretely, of prophet, of *anthrōpos apestalmenos para theou?* As *apestalmenos para theou* the prophet, without being the Logos, assumes the function of the Revealer and to that extent shares his significance and worth. This is a servant's share, a subordinate share — on this see v. 8! — but it is still a share. Inasmuch as he is *apestalmenos para theou* his *gegonenai.* his humanity, his belonging to the created world, and even to the dominion of *skotia.* does not in the slightest prevent him from being seen (as in vv. 9ff.) from the standpoint of the light of revelation that comes into the world from the very first. With reference to him it can be said of the light of redemption, of life, that it was in the world (v. 10) even apart from the epiphany of the Word itself. If it was the Evangelist's concern, even before he began to speak as an Evangelist, to consider and state in principle what he and his fellows were doing in this function relative to its subject, he could hardly do it in a more appropriate way than by the presentation that he initiates in v. 6.

7. **Houtos ēlthen eis martyrian, hina martyrēsę peri tou phōtos, hina pantes pisteusōsin di' autou.** I have already said in the Introduction that this verse should prevent us from viewing the

---

[58]J. Calvin, op. cit., col. 7. [See Eng. tr. p. 13: "[He] appeared in the role rather of an angel than of a man. And so he is not praised for his own abilities, but just because he was the ambassador of God."]

assessment of the Baptist in the prologue one-sidedly from the standpoint of its probable ecclesiastico-political significance and hence interpreting it in a one-sided negative way. In this verse, as H. Holtzmann[59] better perceived than W. Bauer after him,[60] every word but one is positive. And this verse is present and throws light on the whole statement, as v. 8 will in its own fashion later.

Ēlthen is here undoubtedly the same solemn *erchesthai* with which Elijah came according to the Synoptics, the same as that with which the kingdom of God has come near, the same as that with which the Son of Man will come at the end of the days, the same as that which serves both in the Synoptics and in this Gospel to denote the first epiphany of the Lord. "Coming" is also a technical term for the appearing of the Revealer in Mandean works. If the appearance of the Baptist as a total phenomenon (this is the point in v. 7 as distinct from vv. 19ff.) is described by this solemn *erchesthai,* this embraces its coordination with the office of the Revealer himself. The same is true of the terms *martyria* and *martyrein,* which, as we have said in the Introduction, denote also the work of the disciples of Jesus and at times that of Jesus himself. Finally, note how directly the aim of the mission of John is described by the point that all are to believe through him. The above-mentioned exception, the limitation of the positive character of the statement about John, lies in the self-evident *pisteusōsin di' autou.* This at once sets the Baptist alongside the Samaritan woman, of whom it is said in 4:41f. that many come to believe through her word, whereas the Gospel never says that anyone believes "through" Jesus but always that people believe or do not believe *eis auton* or *autǭ.* Consider what this means. One may believe, i.e., come to faith, through John, but the Revealer himself is the object of faith. We have seen the solemn mediatorial significance of the expression *di' autou* in v. 3. What breadth and depth it gives to John's summons to repentance and baptism of repentance — his function according to the Synoptics. It rules out any limitation of his significance as purely Old Testament or perhaps legal (v. 17). The *pantes* shows that his work is both extensive and universal, as that of the Samaritan woman in ch. 4 could never be, and as only that of Christ, and on a lower level that of his disciples as his designated wit-

---

[59]H. J. Holtzmann, op. cit., p. 38.
[60]W. Bauer, op. cit., p. 14.

nesses, can also be. All who come to faith are to do so through John. That is how we are to construe the *pantes,* and later the *phōtizei panta anthrōpon* of v. 9. All this is indeed positive enough. Irrespective of the caveat in v. 8, it is important for the author to say that there is not only the absolute but also a qualified relative, not only revelation but also, deriving from it, relating to it, serving it, applying to all to whom revelation applies, the witness to it, the indication of it, the word from the lips of a man, but from a man who is "sent by God." What *martyria* and *martyrein* are may best be seen if we take as literally as possible the *peri* and genitive with which John's Gospel often denotes the object of witness. Witness is truly and in the best sense speaking *about* a subject, describing it exactly and fully, pointing to it, confirming and repeating it, and all in such a way that the subject remains itself and can speak for itself, that it is not in any way absorbed in human speech or shouted down and overpowered by it. Only where we have supreme concern both to be as close to the subject as possible, and yet to keep at a distance so that it may speak for itself, do we have *martyria.* And *di' autou,* by a human mediator of the divine Mediator, by this human witness that is still qualified as a medium, *di' anthrōpou apestalmenou para theou,* there comes about, not revelation, for this needs no witness in order to take place, but faith in it. *"Testis hic nostra, non Christi causa est ordinatus."*[61] But he *is* ordained for our sake. As we come to faith, we cannot bypass or leap over the witness, the prophet, the apostle. The figure of John is not there for nothing. It is not there for its own sake at the beginning of all the Gospels. In John's Gospel especially the first disciples come to Jesus as they follow the pointing finger of John. "John" in the broadest sense, understood in such a way that the prophets before him and the apostles after him are also "John," as he stands in highly significant ambivalence between them — this John, because he is a relative entity, is not on that account an indifferent or dispensable entity. "L'idée du témoignage [. . .] est corrélative et inséparable de celle de la foi" (F. Godet).[62] From the other side, we may also say with Schlatter: "He who is

---

[61]Cf. J. Calvin, op. cit., col. 7. [See Eng. tr. p. 13: "This witness was ordained, not for Christ's sake but for ours."]

[62]F. Godet, op. cit., p. 59. [See Eng. tr. p. 257: "This idea of *testimony* . . . is correlative and inseparable from that of faith."]

a witness has a right to be believed. He speaks as one who knows about something that others do not know and cannot know for themselves. He tells them so that they may achieve certainty through his knowledge. If in reply to the word of witness faith grasps it and accepts it, then the light shines into us. By whether we come to faith or not it may be seen whether the light wins the victory or shone in the darkness in vain, whether it remained or withdrew."[63] Thus far Schleiermacher rightly observed concerning this verse that "John the Baptist is close to the Redeemer as the instrument that God uses."[64]

8. But now we come very definitely to the caveat with which alone all this can be said. **Ouk ēn ekeinos to phōs, all' hina martyrēsē peri tou phōtos.** Only now, if very vigorously (for note the emphatic place of *ouk ēn*), do we find polemic, not against the Baptist, but against a false evaluation of the Baptist. The Baptist must not be confused with the Revealer; he must be respected in his position as a witness. The existence of a false evaluation of the Baptist is presupposed not only here but also in v. 15, in vv. 19ff., in ch. 3, and elsewhere in the New Testament. Luke 3:15 tells us that the people were musing in their hearts whether John was the Christ. In his address at Antioch Paul has John issue the disclaimer: "I am not the one you suppose me to be" (Acts 13:25). The statement of John that all the Synoptics record (Mark 1:7; Matt. 3:11; Luke 3:16): "A mightier than I comes after me," and the related sayings about the shoelaces and the baptism that is more than water baptism, are also to be understood in connection with this presupposition. The same is true of the doubting question of the Baptist from prison as it is recorded in Matt. 11:3: "Are you he who is to come, or do we look for another?" We are also told in Acts 18:24f. that the Alexandrian Apollos, whom we also know from 1 Corinthians but who was then in Ephesus, was "an eloquent man, well versed in the scriptures, instructed in the way of the Lord, and fervent in spirit," but also that although he *edidasken akribōs ta peri tou Iēsou,* he knew only the baptism of John. And we are then told in Acts 19:1ff. that there were "some disciples" in Ephesus who had never even heard of a Holy Spirit, and who explain this by the fact that they have been baptized only with

---

[63]A. Schlatter, op. cit., p. 4.
[64]F. Schleiermacher, op. cit., p. 18.

John's baptism. This deviation, which the author of Acts obviously judges very mildly and thinks is easily remediable, clearly presupposes both here and in the Synoptics and John an alleged superiority of the Baptist to Christ. This is obvious from what Paul says to these disciples in Acts 19:4: that John taught the people that they should believe in him who was to come after him, namely, in Jesus. Not, then, in John, who plainly stands in the background. Apart from the question in Luke 3:15, the thesis that Jesus is the Christ is presupposed in John 1:20 and 3:28. The New Testament itself never says expressly that such and such people presented and championed this thesis. But the Pseudo-Clementine *Recognitions* in 1.60 tell us: *"Ecce unus ex discipulis Ioannis affirmabat Christum Ioannem fuisse et non Iesum."* ["Behold, one of the disciples of John asserted that John was the Christ and not Jesus."] And the fact that there was a messianic glorifying of the Baptist and hence a related polemic in his favor and against Jesus seems to be confirmed in an interesting way by recent Mandean research. I will quote a remarkable passage from these works as it is given by W. Bauer (op. cit., p. 15): "When John lives in that age of Jerusalem, goes to the Jordan, and baptizes, Jesus Christ comes, goes thither in humility, receives the baptism of John, and is taught by the wisdom of John. But then he twists the words of John, changes baptism in the Jordan, perverts the words of Kušta and preaches wickedness and deception in the world." If it is a long way from the disciples of John in Acts, whose chief representative, Apollos, is so finely eulogized even prior to his Christian baptism, to those whose voice is heard here, there can be no mistaking the fact that the vigor and urgency with which John's Gospel presents the countertithesis seems to point to a very much sharper mood than that presupposed in the disciples of John in Acts 18–19.

No matter how things might have been with the history and structure of this rival church, we obviously have to reckon with a religio-historical and ecclesiastico-political background to this verse. John's Gospel belongs to a specific historical situation, although we can, of course, form only a partial and hypothetical picture of it with the help of occasional inferences. Clearly by no means the least important part of this situation was the need to say that John the Baptist was not the light, not the Christ (1:20; 3:28), not the returning Elijah, not the awaited prophet of later Jewish hopes (1:21), not the bridegroom (3:29), not the one who comes from

above, from heaven (3:31). Vv. 1-5 prepare us for these negations
as they cause us, at least with side-glances, to look around and
consider where we stand. The full deity of the Word (v. 1), the
reference to Jesus (he is the Word, v. 2), the subordination of everything that has come into being to the Word (v. 3), the restriction of
the concept of light or revelation to *the* life that was in the Word
(v. 4), and the opposing of revelation to the darkness as the sphere
in which we human beings live (v. 5) — when we consider the place
of the problem of the Baptist in the prologue, none of these things
can be asserted without the Baptist also being in view. But as we
were careful then not to allow the amply justified side-glance to
lead us to neglect the far richer content of the presentation in which
those references are embedded, so now, when the red thread is
plain to see and takes a central place in the text itself, we must
be careful not to see in the text only the practical historical
background. In modern exposition that inclines in this direction the
text takes on a remarkably petty and spiteful character that the
author would not have tolerated. All honor to the Mandeans and
all that is connected with them! But the possible correction of the
squabblings of a Near Eastern sect is not the only thing or the final
thing that we must see here.

We should certainly remember that any criticism there might
be here either of the Baptist or of a sect of the Baptist has universal
and typical significance for the author. In putting the witness in his
place he surely recalls that he himself could have only the function
of a witness, so that all that he wrote about the Baptist was automatically written about himself as well. In principle the same
misunderstanding or confusion to which he sees the sect of the
Baptist fall victim is the danger that besets every witness of the
light. Luther was undoubtedly right when he said of this verse that
the world suffers from the affliction of being full of masters and
know-alls, of sages and lights, who seek their own way to heaven
and want to be lights of the world and teach and lead us how to
come to God; John is warning us against such.[65] Wherever we have
this confusion, the witness, instead of remaining a witness, begins
to pose as the Revealer, points to himself instead of to Christ, and

---

[65]M. Luther, *Auslegung des ersten und zweiten Kapitels Johannis in Pre-
digten 1537 und 1538*. WA 46, p. 584 (quoted from C. G. Eberle, p. 87; see n. 39
above). [See Eng. tr. pp. 56f. (cited in n. 39 above).]

makes God's cause his own. And wherever, as commonly happens, the disciples of the witness, out of pure gratitude and enthusiasm, do him the wrong of putting him in a place where he does not belong (although probably in a more refined way than in that Mandean text), there John 1:8 is apposite, for there we have a sect of the Baptist which cannot be too plainly or sharply refuted. The practical historical background of the text should not cause us to lose sight of the universal and typical nature of the problem that it raises.

A second point is even more definite and important. We have stressed from the very outset that the criticism of the Baptist is positive, i.e., that the No carries with it dialectically a Yes which is openly and non-dialectically expressed and which is thus to be heard no less attentively. We distort the meaning of the text if with W. Bauer[66] we put an "only" in brackets before the *eis martyrian* (v. 7) and the *hina martyrēsē* (v. 8). A witness who is really a witness, from all that we have heard in vv. 6-7, is not "only" a witness. In doing justice to the polemical element in the verse we have to allow that the "only" has some validity, but in reading and interpreting v. 8 in context, with vv. 6-7 preceding it and vv. 9ff. following, we have no reason to view it merely as polemic, vigorous though the polemic may be. The second and positive part of the statement is certainly not just an amplification of the first and negative part, where Bauer's "only" would be in place (although not in a translation). The second part is related in content to vv. 6-7, which are so positive that no one would think of limiting them by an "only" were it not for v. 8a. What they say is already limited and needs no further limitation. All that is said in vv. 6-7, within the limitation, applies also to what is said in v. 8a. Because the Baptist is not the light he is no less what he is and can be, a witness. What v. 8a affirms in definition of the term "witness" is the servant-relationship, the subordination, the dependence which applies to the one thus named over against revelation. But what vv. 6-7 affirm on behalf of v. 8b is that being a witness (even if *only* a witness) means a positive share [in revelation][67] even if this share be only indirect and on a lower level. John the Baptist is a mountain peak which is visible in the valley and which is lit up by

---

[66]W. Bauer, op. cit., pp. 14f.
[67]Added from A.

the morning sun when the sun is not yet seen in the valley. The comparison is once again Augustine's. Augustine tells us — strikingly with reference to v. 9 — that John the Baptist came to weak spirits, to sick hearts, to the enfeebled eyes of the soul. This is why he came. And how could the soul see what is perfect? In the same way, as often happens, one can see the risen sun on an object on which it shines when one cannot see the sun with the eyes. For even those who have weak eyes can see a wall which is lit up and illumined by the sun, or they can see a mountain or a tree or some other object, and in another object the sun shows that it has risen even when they have no ability to see it for themselves. In the same way all those for whom Christ came were not completely unable to see him. He lit up John, and through him, who confessed that he was illumined and enlightened but did not himself illumine or enlighten, he was known who illumines, enlightens, and fills.[68] Like Augustine, we are certainly not deviating from the Evangelist's meaning if we say that John the Baptist represents a whole category here. What is true of him is true of all those who with him, classically represented by him, fall under the concept of "witness." Hence in what follows in vv. 9ff. when we read of the *phōs erchomenon eis ton kosmon,* we are not to think only of the direct light of the incarnate Word which will be expressly mentioned only in v. 14. Implicitly, of course, there is reference to this too in vv. 9-13, as we had to assume that there was already in v. 5. But along with the direct light there is also for John an indirect light of revelation, which, as we noted already in v. 5, even now as dawn, or indeed as the half-light of midnight, is light from the same light even when its source, the sun, is not yet visible in the sky. This is what seems to be in view in vv. 9-13, which precede the saying about the Incarnation, if there is some significance in the fact that the saying about the Incarnation comes at the end and not at the beginning. And in vv. 9-13 John the Baptist undoubtedly is not the only one at issue. He represents all those who can and must be mentioned with reference to the *phōs erchomenon eis ton kosmon* in this derived and secondary sense. If this anticipated understanding of vv. 9ff. later proves to be correct, then v. 8 also has a forward reference. As the bearer of this indirect, broken, and muffled light,

---

[68]Augustine, op. cit., II, 7 (pp. 23f.). [See Eng. tr. pp. 15f.]

as the reflector of the light itself, as the representative of Advent who can be present only because Christmas comes, as the one who is reached already by the revelation of life in the midst of the field of force of darkness, as the one who gives information about this revelation, he is what he is, the witness, and over against the Revealer the first of those of whom there is to be said what vv. 12-13 will tell us about "those who received him," the proclaimer of what he himself has known to those who have not yet known it, and for this reason also the one who has to draw back when he hears the voice of the bridegroom (3:29), the one who must decrease because the latter increases (3:30). In the same way, as the sun rises one no longer looks at the mountain peak which is lit up by it. The light of Christmas is the end of the lights of Advent. When the building is complete, the scaffolding can fall. When the subject itself speaks, there is no longer any need to speak about it, *peri tou phōtos.* This is the limit, the "only," the restriction under which the witness stands as such. But within this limit he is what he is with authority and power.

We can meaningfully relate all this to the witnesses of revelation both *before* and *after* the epiphany. Before the epiphany John sees the Old Testament, concerning which he says in 8:56 the most unheard-of thing, which one has to read in connection with the New Testament. After the epiphany there is the church, within which he himself has a part. He finds light, the light that comes into the world, both before and after, both *before* the great *skēnoun* of the Logos among us (v. 14) and *after* his *poreuein,* his departure, among whose signs the later chapters of the Gospel are to be numbered. John the Baptist stands for him on the knife-edge border as the last to bear witness to him who is to come and the first to bear witness to him who has already come, already in some sense looking back to him when he calls him the Lamb of God that takes away the sin of the world [1:29]. Hence he and his position have both positively and negatively a universal[69] significance that embraces the different times. In this regard note the *ēn* of v. 8a with a reference back to v. 4. In this light we take it that the *pisteusōsin di' autou* of v. 7 means that all in some way must pass by him and his pointing finger if they are to come to faith. Hence the compar-

---

[69]A puts "supratemporal" before "universal."

ison of the epiphany to the rising sun has its limits. We are not to press it historically as though the position and character of the witness became different after the years 1 to 30 from what they were before. All witness to revelation is as such the Advent message, not *phōs* but *martyria peri tou phōtos*. At all times and in all circumstances the bearer of the Christmas message, having his own light, is the Word that is incarnate in the fulness of time. But the witnesses of the remotest past and the most distant future have in principle a similar share in revelation, or render a similar service to it. There applies to all of them the caveat that in themselves, if they do not misunderstand themselves, they are only witnesses, only friends of the bridegroom, destined to decrease, not worthy to untie his shoelaces. One may put more stress on either the positive or the negative side. At different times one or the other may be more necessary. That is not important. The important thing is that the office of the witness, the ministering function in relation to Christ, should be seen and understood as a function that there *always* has been and always *again* has to be, for our sake, not Christ's,[70] as a reflection of his own function.

9. **Ēn to phōs to alēthinon, ho phōtizei panta anthrōpon, erchomenon eis ton kosmon.** We have first to consider the understanding of older exegesis, and today not only of Schlatter[71] but also of E. Schwartz,[72] which also found expression in, e.g., Luther's translation: "That was the true light that lights all men that come into this world." On this view the subject lies outside the sentence and is best sought in the preceding *phōs*. *Erchomenon eis ton kosmon* then goes with *anthrōpon*, and the stress obviously falls on *panta*; everybody that comes into the world is illumined by the true light. Taken in connection with vv. 10-11 (according to H. J. Holtzmann's formulation), what we have is thus a complaint "that men still need a witness to the same Logos when it has already been so close to every one of them."[73] Opinions differ as to whether the light that comes into the world is to be regarded as the grace that has always

---

[70]See n. 61.

[71]A. Schlatter, op. cit., p. 4.

[72]E. Schwartz, "Aporien im 4. Evangelium," *Nachrichten von der königlichen Gesellschaft der Wissenschaften zu Göttingen* (1908), p. 532 n. 1, quoted from W. Bauer, op. cit., p. 16.

[73]H. J. Holtzmann, op. cit., p. 38.

been offered to all (Augustine, Luther, Schlatter)[74] or the *communis lux naturae* (Calvin), i.e., the *sensus aeternae lucis* which is given to each of us with reason and conscience, which is spoiled by the fall, but which still cannot be lost or destroyed in substance.[75] Linguistically this view has in its favor the undeniable fact that it makes the order of the sentence easier to understand, but it has against it the lack of a subject in the sentence, the subject having to be supplied, not very convincingly, from what precedes: *to phōs ēn to phōs to alēthinon, ho phōtize.* . . . Materially it has in its favor the excellent forward connection, at least up to v. 11, but against it stands the arbitrariness of the link with vv. 6-8, as though there were some reason to bewail the need for a special witness to the light. With most modern exegetes I think the arguments against this reading carry the day. Favoring the reading: "The light was coming into the world,"[76] which Cocceius, too, vigorously supported,[77] is the linguistic point that the author likes to use what is called the periphrastic imperfect (cf. 1:28; 3:23; 10:40, *ēn baptizōn*; etc.; examples collected by W. Bauer).[78] Again, "coming into the world" is constantly in this Gospel a function of the light or of Jesus (cf. 3:19; 12:46; etc.), in agreement with a Mandean formula and contrary to Philo, in whom God keeps the Logos with himself.[79] Finally (a point made by H. J. Holtzmann),[80] a fine contrast results between the surprisingly placed *ēn,* followed at once by the subject *phōs.* and the *ouk ēn* of v. 8. We thus translate: "The true light, which lights every man, was coming into the world."

But what does this mean? First, what is *to phōs to alēthinon*? Four related meanings for *alēthinos* call for consideration: (1) "genuine" as distinct from false, imitative, or only apparently corresponding to the concept; (2) close to, or coincident with, *alēthēs.* i.e., "related to or filled with the truth," "belonging to the realm of truth";[81] (3) "reliable," "credible"; (4) "true" in the sense

---

[74]Augustine, op. cit., II, 7 (p. 24) [see Eng. tr. pp. 15f.]; M. Luther, WA 10, 1. pp. 220ff. [see Eng. tr. pp. 66ff. (cited in n. 39 above)]; Schlatter, op. cit., pp. 4f.

[75]Calvin, op. cit, col. 9. [See Eng. tr. p. 15.]

[76]B has "had come" (perhaps a mistake in dictation).

[77]J. Cocceius, op. cit., p. 11.

[78]W. Bauer, op. cit., p. 17.

[79]Quoted in W. Bauer, op. cit., p. 17.

[80]H. J. Holtzmann, op. cit., p. 38.

[81]W. Bauer, loc. cit.

of the reality that has only an original and not a copy; cf. the true
and heavenly tabernacle of Heb. 8:2 which God has set up and not
man. If we look at other passages in the Gospel in which the term
occurs, we have to say that according to the context pretty well all
the meanings are more or less possible in their own place. As for
this passage, in context I decide (with Calvin)[82] for the fourth possibility. There can be no question here of opposition to a false or
imitation light, for John the Baptist is not regarded as such. The
meaning "related to the truth" is so general that its colorlessness
and abstractness make a strange impression in this verse. The
sense "reliable" or "trustworthy" fits well enough if the thought of
the illumination of men by the light is the real point of the statement. But from what we have just said it is not. The paraphrase
of Calvin makes good sense. Light in heaven and earth always
receives its radiance from elsewhere. But Christ is the light which
shines of itself and then fills the whole world with *its* radiance:
*"ut non alia sit usquam origo vel causa splendoris. Veram ergo
lucem dixit, cui natura proprium est lucere."* ["There is no other
source or cause of its brightness anywhere. And so he calls Him
the true light whose own nature is to be light."] Over against the
witness *peri tou phōtos* there stood and stands the *phōs alēthinon,*
the original, uncreated, primary light, the direct and immediate
revelation of life that bears witness to itself. Of this true light a
relative clause tells us: *ho phōtizei panta anthrōpon. Phōtizein* is
more than *phainein* (v. 5), and the relative clause says more than
v. 4b (that the light was the life of men). Not just an activity but
an effect of light is meant here. It illumines men, it fills them with
light, it sets them in the light. To the extent that they are set in the
light at all! *"Quisquis illuminatur, ab hac luce illuminatur."*[83] It is
in this restrictive sense that we are to take the *panta,* after the
analogy of the *pantes* of v. 7. Everyone who receives light receives
it from this source. Obviously also the man mentioned in v. 6! Only
in this way and to this extent does he himself shed light so that
others come to faith through him — only as he is illumined by this

---

[82]Calvin, op. cit., col. 8. [See Eng. tr. p. 14.]

[83]J. A. Bengel, *Gnomon Novi Testamenti,* vol. I, 2nd ed. (Tübingen, 1850),
p. 360. [See the English translation by A. R. Fausset, *Gnomon of the New Testament,* vol. II (Edinburgh, 1877), p. 244: "whosoever is enlightened at all, is
enlightened by this Light."]

true and primary light. By this light which is first original and then alone at work, is what the author means to say. Of this light he says that it was *erchomenon eis ton kosmon,* i.e., coming into the world. What does this mean? According to Cocceius, H. Holtzmann, Heitmüller, and Zahn,[84] we must quietly supply a *tote* before *erchomenon.* According to this view the Evangelist's meaning is then that "when the Baptist witnessed to him, Jesus began to emerge from the concealment of his former life" (Zahn). Against this view it has been repeatedly pointed out that in spite of the "there was" with which they begin, vv. 6-8 (cf. v. 15, and in contrast v. 19) are not a historical account or record but the evaluation and characterization of a concrete historical entity to which it would be most inappropriate to attach the story of the coming of Jesus (which in this case would be just as oddly abstract as, one has to say, Zahn's view of v. 4 is). No, the reference is not to the light which appeared in the humanity of Jesus, although not first or only in this humanity, but to the primary light of the revelation of life from which all other light derives (with the Baptist, and the category that he represents, in view). This light was (the same time-embracing *ēn* as in v. 4 and v. 8) *coming* into the world. Later in v. 10 we shall read that it was in the world. Here we have the explanation that we also found in v. 4. The *being* of this light in the world is its *coming.* But its coming in full reality! This coming establishes the truth of what is said about the Baptist in vv. 6-8. Because the primary light is coming into the world there is a Baptist, a *martyria.* Not in virtue of the *erchesthai* of such men (v. 7) but in virtue of the *erchesthai,* the dawn, of the light, of which their *erchesthai* on the lower level, in history, gives intimation — not out of the caprice of religious yearning but out of the necessity which is laid upon them by the inconceivable divine condescension which is enacted again and again in this coming.

10. En tō kosmō ēn — kai ho kosmos di' autou egeneto — kai ho kosmos auton ouk egnō. The structure of this verse reminds us strikingly of v. 1: three short statements joined by *kai* and all three rotating around a single concept, in this case *kosmos.* If we note the masculine *auton* in the third statement, and if we assume, as

---

[84]Cocceius, op. cit., pp. 11-12; H. J. Holtzmann, op. cit., p. 39; W. Heitmüller, "Das Johannes-Evangelium," *Die Schriften des Neuen Testaments,* vol. II (Göttingen, 1907), 3, p. 194; T. Zahn, op. cit., p. 70.

is probable, that this same masculine is the subject in the first statement, and after the analogy of v. 3 is also meant in the *di᾿ autou* of the second, then we see that the masculine can refer only to the *ho logos* of vv. 1ff. and v. 14 (unless with Zahn[85] we look ahead and seek to refer it at once to the historical Jesus). There thus arises unsought a material parallel as well to v. 1. Comparison shows that between them we have come a considerable way. With the same urgency with which v. 1 taught the deity[86] of the Word, v. 10 now teaches its turning to the world. With the necessary caution one might say that the former refers to the transcendence of the Logos, the latter to its immanence in the world. It is important to note, however, that the *en tǭ kosmǭ ēn* of this verse understands the immanence as an event in contrast to permanent immanence. V. 9, and further back v. 5, and also v. 11 with its *ēlthen*, forbid us to construe this *ēn* as a continuous relation. It is act or action. "The Word gave itself to be received by the world," we might paraphrase the first statement. How far the Word was engaged in this turning to the world vv. 4-5 and v. 9 have shown in a general way. Life or redemption was in the Word, and this life was light, it was manifest among men in the midst of the darkness in which they live; it came and comes into the world. How concretely? Vv. 6-8 have given the answer to this question. It came and comes in the form of the witness who is not himself the light of the world but who is its witness with full authority. The term *light*, having rendered this service, recedes into the background. In its place, preparing the ground for v. 14, the Word itself returns as whose life, or redeeming content, the light was introduced. Thus a line is drawn under what goes before. As the light shone (v. 5) and came into the world (v. 9) (the light that was simply the light of *his* life), the Word himself was in the world.

The term *kosmos* can have at least three meanings in John: (1) "The sum of all created things." This meaning fits the second statement best (cf. v. 3). But in the third statement the *kosmos* is depicted as either knowing or not knowing. And all that precedes and follows points to a more specialized meaning for this central concept. (2) "The creature in its hardened turning from God and his revelation," shut off from revelation because it shuts itself off;

---

[85]Zahn, op. cit., p. 72.
[86]B has *Gottheit*. A *Göttlichkeit*.

the world as per se the world that lies in the evil one [cf. 1 John 5:19b]. This pregnant meaning, which is common in John, fits the content of the third statement very well — but perhaps too well inasmuch as the statement then becomes analytic. And v. 11 shows that the author does not regard the world as from the very outset alien and hostile but wants to depict its turning from the Word as an unexpected and scandalous episode. (If we adopt these first two meanings, we have to assume that there is a shift of meaning in the middle of the verse. The world that came into being through the Word could not be the world that is hardened, and the world that does not know the Word could not be simply the sum of all that is created. Such a change of meaning is not impossible in John, but it is perhaps as well not to use the resultant exegetical possibility too hastily or too often.) (3) "The human world," "homines in mundo,"[87] "the earth and the people on it,"[88] history as a world within the world. With this sense *kosmos* would be neutral in the first two statements, its sense being determined by its relation to the Word, this sense then being found in the third statement. I regard this third sense as the most probable in the context, especially in the light of the third statement and the related v. 11. If we want to assume a shift of meaning, then we have sense (1) in the first and second statements and sense (3) in the third. Our interpretation is thus as follows.

1. *En tǭ kosmǭ ēn.* The Word neither was nor is remote from humanity. His life, which is their redemption, became and is manifest. It could and can be received. Care is taken that no one has to feel left out. No one can complain of unfair treatment. The witness and testimony to him are there. "Their voice goes out through all the earth" [Ps. 19:4]. Calvin paraphrases: *"Summa est, nunquam talem fuisse Christi absentiam a mundo, quin homines eius radiis expergefacti in ipsum attollere oculos debuerint."*[89] Those who have ears to hear, let them hear!

2. *Kai ho kosmos di' autou egeneto.* If we have correctly ex-

---

[87]Cocceius, op. cit., p. 13.

[88]J. L. von Mosheim, *Erklärung des Evangelii Johannis,* ed. A. F. E. Jakobi, (Weimar, 1777), p. 10.

[89]Calvin, op. cit., cols. 9f. [See Eng. tr. pp. 15f.: "The sum of it is that Christ was never so absent from the world that men ought not to have been awakened by His rays and to have looked up to Him."]

pounded the parallel in v. 3, here again the stress lies on the fact that over against the human world the Word has all the superiority of the Creator. It was not a part of the human world. It came into the world from above, from heaven, as will later be said of Christ [3:31], from that which is in principle above all that has come into being, yet not, of course, as a foreign body, but as the truth (v. 11 may be heard in advance in this second statement in v. 10) which the world really ought to know. If it came in the form of human witness to it, even in the reflection of this witness it was no less *to phōs to alēthinon* (v. 9). the primary light that no one may rightly evade.

3. *Ho kosmos auton ouk egnō.* In view of the continuation in v. 11 one can hardly miss the fact that the two preceding statements are written for the sake of this statement. Here again and in relation to v. 11 reference has been made[90] to the "impression of tragedy in the life of Jesus" to which these statements allude. But if the concept of tragedy cannot be separated from the element of fateful guilt or guilty fate in the hero, then if there is tragedy here, in the mind of the Evangelist the cosmos rather than Jesus is the tragic hero who, the captive of fate and guilt, finally misses the supreme opportunity that is offered. V. 10c and v. 11 certainly raise such a complaint and accusation against the cosmos, although in the mind of the Evangelist the complaint and accusation hardly have a "tragic" ring in the pregnant sense of the term. Not unjustifiably, perhaps, we are reminded by the verse of the pessimistic judgment on the cosmos that we also find in Hermetic and Mandean writings. But we have to add at once that this judgment does not harden into a dualistic system in John. Note the significance of the fact that v. 10c is embedded between v. 10b and v. 11. We have here a momentary part of the situation of conflict similar to that found in v. 5. We do not have a metaphysical principle. One may thus ask whether the complaint and accusation can really be called the true purpose of the passage vv. 10c-11. Note the connection of the passage with vv. 12-13. Quite indisputably these verses depict a mighty deed of the Word. Among those who contest it, the Word itself gives a great number, the *hosoi.* the possibility or power for something unheard-of and humanly impossible, i.e., for being God's *children* (really

---

[90]W. Bauer, op. cit., p. 17.

God's children according to the strict interpretation of v. 13) in the midst of a crooked generation [Phil. 2:15]. One cannot deny that the paradox of v. 11 effectively prepares the way for the depiction of this mighty deed of the Word. This is how the Word worked and works by its own power. It is not heard by those by whom it ought to be heard and yet — wholly by itself — it has found receptivity and faith. On the other hand, one cannot deny that v. 11 is only the explication of v. 10c. Hence one cannot allow v. 10c, or v. 10 as a whole, or with it v. 11, to be regarded only as that complaint about the world or that accusation against it. Beyond this note, which is certainly present but only as a secondary note, there sounds as the meaning of the whole passage vv. 9-13 the melody of triumph as the Word, the true and only effective light (v. 9), comes into the world, inconceivably finds no echo in the world, and yet equally inconceivably — enigma again confronts enigma as in v. 5 — completes its work in the world in spite of the world, reaches its goal, finds faith, and gives birth to children of God. Even though it is present to the world in the dignity of the Creator, it meets only with resistance in it. Like what is said in v. 5 (that it shines in isolation, in the darkness which does not comprehend it, but that it still finds its witness in the sphere of darkness, that by its power and deed it still finds open ears in the world that resists it), this truth shames the world and brings blame upon it and complaint against it. Yet again we must not make the Evangelist stop there. We must not find in him only an attitude of what might be called theological pettiness in face of the world. The church's right to judge the world depends upon the judgment not being a last word but having only subordinate significance. And this is what it has in this passage. What the Evangelist says about the world is not said for its own sake but for the glorifying of the Word, which, although it is not received by men, sees to it that nevertheless it is received, because it has the power to give *exousia* where none exists. To this goal, which is intimated in v. 9, we have taken the first step in v. 10.

11. Eis ta idia ēlthen, kai hoi idioi auton ou parelabon. This is at all events a closer definition of v. 10a and v. 10b as well as v. 10c. We have here figurative language. If with Luther and many others we take *ta idia* to mean "possession," this makes exposition so much easier, for figure and reality are then congruent. But *ta idia* probably has the more concrete sense of "home" or "homeland,"

and in this case *hoi idioi* are relatives or compatriots. It is clear
that one cannot press the comparison but must take it with a pinch
of salt. The world is naturally not the home of the Logos, as though
he came from it, and men are not his compatriots, as though he
were one of them. The point of comparison is the original and intimate relationship in which he who comes from afar stands to this
place and its inhabitants. He belongs to it and to them by right.
They ought to receive him willingly and joyfully as one who is at
home with them. For they themselves belong originally to him.
They ought to see that they stand in an original relationship to him.
But they do not. The absurd thing stated in v. 10c takes place and
becomes an event. Although the Logos came where he truly belonged, even if as one apart, according to v. 3 and v. 10, those who
were there, his own people, did not receive him, as though his claim
were not natural, legitimate, factual, and self-evident. In exposition
there is debate as to who or what we are to understand by the *ta
idia* and *hoi idioi*. Decision is not easy. According to Augustine,
Calvin, Cocceius, Zahn, and Harnack,[91] we are to think of the
people of Israel, of the Jews as those predestined to be the special
recipients of revelation both from ancient times and again obviously
in the epiphany. In this case the passage is a parallel to the parable
of the wicked husbandmen in Matt. 21 [Matt. 21:33-41]. But I
prefer to go with the view of H. Holtzmann, W. Heitmüller, and
W. Bauer,[92] who lay their fingers on the point that this thought
would be strangely isolated and unmotivated and unfruitful in this
context even though it might agree well with what the Gospel says
elsewhere about the Jews and even though it would offer an effective crescendo from v. 10 to v. 11. This interpretation is alien to the
context, and it is more appropriate to take *ta idia* and *hoi idioi* as
characterizing the human world as a whole. The Word is not alien
in the world; this thought of v. 10a and v. 10b is now taken up in
more precise form, still with a reference to what is there called
kosmos, but with a stronger emphasis on the fact that the cosmos

---

[91]Augustine, op. cit., II, 12 (p. 27) [see Eng. tr. p. 17]; Calvin, op. cit.,
col. 10 [see Eng. tr. p. 16]; Cocceius, op. cit., p. 14; Zahn, op. cit., p. 73; A. Harnack,
"Über das Verhältnis des Prologs des vierten Evangeliums zum ganzen Werk,"
Zeitschrift für Theologie und Kirche, 2 (1892), 189-231, esp. p. 220.
[92]Holtzmann, op. cit., p. 14; Heitmüller, op. cit., p. 194; Bauer, op. cit.,
p. 19.

belongs to the Logos. The Word belongs to the cosmos in the same
way — we must stress the element of comparison — as one who has
resided abroad for a long time belongs to his homeland and is eo
ipso at home there when he returns. For the world belongs to him,
we must rightly add. Perhaps literally with Justin: *Hou pan genos
anthrōpōn meteschen.*[93] or, in another passage, *Pantes anthrōpoi
. . . logikoi . . . gegenēntai.*[94] The figure of *ta idia* and *hoi idioi*
serves to underline the *en tǭ kosmǭ ēn* of v. 10. He came where he
could and should come. His coming could not mean anything new
or strange. Along the same lines the *ou parelabon* is a sharpening
of the *ouk egnō* of v. 10; there took place that which could not and
should not possibly take place. In this verse, as in v. 2, we must
perhaps make a concession to Zahn's view, forced though it may
be as a whole. H. Holtzmann, already in relation to v. 7, may not
be wrong when he says that the *ēlthen* refers to a single coming,
a historical fact.[95] In this case the totality of the coming of the true
light into the world, the revelatory being of the Word in it, becomes
in this passage, which gives the relation pointed expression, in a
quiet anticipation of v. 14, the great once-for-all historical "he came,"
the manifestation of the primary shining light in person at a single
moment. This is where the emphasis significantly lies, as in the
houtos of v. 2. Why should this not be so? It is also possible that
the concrete *ēlthen* which gives rise to this interpretation is simply
governed by the concrete figure of the one who returns to his homeland and that materially it does not have any significance beyond
that of the *ēn erchomenon* of v. 9. However that may be, the situation depicted more generally in v. 10 is sharpened in v. 11. The
human world, created by the Word, destined for it, and belonging
to it, is the Word's own (as we must definitely say echoing the freer
translation of Luther). Yet it does not hear and receive the Word in
such a way that faith and obedience are found it it.

**12-13. Hosoi de elabon auton, edōken autois exousian, tekna
theou genesthai, tois pisteuousin eis to onoma autou, hoi ouk ex**

---

[93]Justin Martyr, *Apology* I. 46 (quoted in Holtzmann, op. cit., p. 40). [See
the English translation by A. Robertson and J. Donaldson, rev. A. C. Coxe, *The
Apostolic Fathers, Justin Martyr, Irenaeus. The Ante-Nicene Fathers*, vol. I (repr.
Grand Rapids, 1975), p. 178.]
[94]*Apology* I, 28 (quoted in Holtzmann, loc. cit.). [See Eng. tr. p. 172.]
[95]H. Holtzmann, op. cit., p. 40.

haimaton oude ek thelēmatos sarkos oude ek thelēmatos andros all'
ek theou egennēthēsan. Can the world sustain its defiance? Is the
Word spoken or witnessed to in vain? Can the world shut out the
Word? Will not God mock it [cf. Gal. 6:7]? An answer is now given
to these questions. Vv. 12-13 form a first climax in the prologue.
If it were a matter of dividing the prologue, I would make a break
at this point, after v. 13. What comes after in vv. 14ff. forms a
second section like a basalt hill rising directly on the plain alongside
the first mountaintop: "The word became flesh" — this is something
more and something different, something new compared to the fact
that it was in the beginning with God, superior to all that came
into being, the bearer of redemption, whose light lightens the world,
which is attested to in the world, which comes into the world in
spite of the whole world. Before this new and different thing can
be said, that train of thought is brought to a conclusion in vv. 12-13.
The opposition, the inconceivable fact that the world is closed to
the Word and its light, is not a final insight in the framework of
that presentation in which there is only a distant reference to the
epiphany. We are not merely to say of the human world that the
darkness did not comprehend the light, that the world did not know
the Logos, that his own did not receive him. There has also to be
said the further and positive thing which comes into the world like
a miracle, the inconceivable reality which finally and definitively
confounds it, namely, that he gives to some the possibility of becoming the children of God. There were and are those who indeed
live in the world like all the rest but who receive him, who believe
in his name, and who in so doing show that in principle the darkness, the hostility of the cosmos, is opposed and defeated. They do
not do this by their own strength or deed, but because their existence when they do so has its origin totally and directly in God
himself and nothing else. When we ask what becomes of the speaking of the divine Word or the shining of the divine light in the dark
world, what success or effect it has, the Evangelist's answer to this
question is[96] that those who are born of God, as those who in their
existence represent a new birth in the ancient world, which the
world and they themselves as world are quite unable to accomplish,
that such people know the Word, receive it, believe in his name.

---

[96]A adds: "(for him as an Evangelist, a witness, it can be only a question
of secondary rank)."

They do this by the *exousia* that is given to them, as those who are born of God.[97] The divinely effected existence of these believers is the answer to the question whether the world can hold out and close itself to the Word. The divinely effected existence of believers replies that the world cannot do so, that the Word is mightier than the world. But only the existence of believers, and this only as divinely effected, makes this reply. There is no answer at all alongside this wholly "actual" answer. On the basis of this actuality John can only say, at the beginning and at the end and in the middle of his Gospel, that light and darkness are in a highly unequal if just as highly incomprehensible conflict. The decision in this conflict falls with the divinely effected existence of those who by their receiving of the Word, by their believing in his name, show that they are *in* this world but not *of* this world, as John 17 will say. This is how I would briefly and provisionally sum up the content of these verses. Let us see whether this view proves to be right in detail.

The relative clause *hosoi de elabon auton* has the character and role of a nominative absolute such as we find in striking fashion in, e.g., 7:38; 8:45; 17:2b. A smooth translation would take it as a dative: "To as many as . . . ," although this expunges the emphasis on the event: *hosoi elabon*. which is what the nominative expression in Greek achieves. *Hosoi* denotes a certain number of entities that are distinguished by a common definition or destiny. Their number does not have to be very small, so that there is no occasion for the observation of W. Bauer: "True religion is always the affair of a little company."[98] The only point of the *hosoi* is that it marks a transition from consideration of all *anthrōpoi*. of the cosmos. of the humanity that v. 11 claims as the *idioi* of the Logos, to a consideration of specific people, of concrete individuals. We are not to see in the change from *parelabon* (v. 11) to *elabon* (v. 12) any shift of nuance (as Zahn does).[99] *Paralambanein*. which in Paul is a technical term for receiving true teaching about Christ based on legitimate tradition, occurs elsewhere in John only twice [14:3; 19:16] and not with the same meaning as here. Nothing

---

[97]A interposes here the sentence: "Every possible answer is enclosed for John in this answer."
[98]W. Bauer, op. cit., p. 19.
[99]T. Zahn, op. cit., p. 73.

special is to be gleaned from *lambanein* in these verses. Inasmuch as it denotes a spiritual process, in John as in the rest of the New Testament it is a regular expression for the willing and responsive acceptance of Jesus, his Word, his witness, or his Spirit. It acquires its special emphasis here from the fact that it is parallel to the *ginōskein* of v. 10. The world of which it is said there, *ouk egnō*, did not do this, it did not receive the Word, it did not appropriate the Word, it neither could nor would see that it was ordained and adapted to do so. It regarded the Word as a foreign body — it did not just regard it as such but treated it as such (for *ginōskein*, interpreted by *lambanein*, obviously denotes an action), when in fact, as v. 11 shows, it was not a foreign body in the world. And now conversely we must interpret *lambanein* or *paralambanein* by *ginōskein*. The revelation of redemptive life demands that people be open, that they be ready for perception; the light that shines demands an eye that sees, the spoken Word demands receptivity, reason. This receptive knowing is what is denoted by *lambanein*. To receive the Word is to let it apply to oneself. Thus *lambanein* leads from *ginōskein* to *pisteuein*, of which we shall speak later.

Whether *ginōskein* is put above or below *pisteuein* in John is hard to say. Perhaps both are true. Knowing is the basic act of discovery which always precedes faith as an attitude or *habitus*, but which always follows it too, both opening it up and also crowning it. Between the two, or comprehensively above them, there obviously stands *lambanein*, in which people recognize and treat revelation as something that is meant for them and directed to them, in which they let themselves be found by it, realizing that they can do no other, that they have already been found by it. They act as *idioi* in fulfilment of that which is theirs essentially as citizens of the world (v. 11). Appropriating the Word is the point of this action, and one might just as well find it described as either the way from knowledge to faith or the way from faith to knowledge, for when such people know, they receive so as to believe, and when they believe, they receive so as to know. *Ginōskein* is enlightenment, *pisteuein* is brightness, and *lambanein* is the aptness of the subject for both these experiences, which cannot be distinguished chronologically. *Hosoi elabon auton* thus signifies an *event*. There are those who are *lambanontes*, receivers, people of "reason," relative to the Word. For them the Word has not just come into the world. Coming into the world, it has properly, as it must, come to

them. They are its *idioi* who see themselves as such. They have
known and they come to believe. They have believed and they come
to know. Within the world the Evangelist sees a pure miracle: these
hosoi. "*De immundis et profanis hic loquitur, qui perpetua igno-
minia damnati, in mortis tenebris iacebant.*"[100] How did they come
to be different from others? Here as always in vv. 1-13 we have to
think of people in all ages of whom it is said that, although they
are in the world and are themselves the world, they do something
that the world and others who are in it do not do; they receive the
Word as though they were not in the world or were not the world.
How do they come to do it?

The main clause in v. 12b supplies the answer: *edōken autois
exousian*. This is an indirect answer. Strictly we have to say that
the three clauses of v. 12 are parallel: "Those who received him —
he gave to them the possibility of becoming God's children — to them
that believe in his name." Only the continuation in v. 13 shows
unmistakably that the main clause *edōken autois* is really the main
clause materially, the central pillar which carries the whole and to
which the dependent clauses on the right hand and on the left must
be materially related. He gave them the possibility *tekna theou
genesthai*. Let us take this first! As these *hosoi* receive the Word,
as they believe in his name according to the later amplification and
interpretation, they are put in a position in which they may become
God's children. By no means arbitrarily we think of Rom. 8:14:
hosoi gar pneumati theou agontai, houtoi huioi theou eisin. The
passage in John is a little more restrained than Paul is there. The
expression *tekna theou* occurs in only one other place in John's
Gospel, i.e., in 11:52, where it is used only incidentally. The expression is more common in 1 John. The synonymous *huioi theou* does
not occur in John at all, although once we find *huioi phōtos* (12:36).
John seems to put the stress in the expression on the fact that those
thus named, although they are men, precisely as such find themselves even within the world in a most promising relationship to
God. Concrete individuals are concretely named and concretely distinguished from others: *tekna theou*. We are this and we are called
this, *klēthōmen kai esmen*, as 1 John 3:1 energetically affirms. "A

---

[100]Calvin, op. cit., col. 11. [See Eng. tr. p. 17: "For here he is speaking of
the unclean and profane who, condemned to perpetual disgrace, lay cast in death's
darkness."]

most promising relationship," I said just above. In 1 John 3:2, in spite of the *esmen*, the expression has about it something provisional. The fulfilment is not yet present. It has not yet appeared what we shall be: *ti esometha*. Are we then to understand the *genesthai* in the present verse eschatologically? Or does it point to the concreteness of the expression notwithstanding the reserve? Can one become a child of God as one might become something else? The last view is the most probable. We are perhaps to take *genesthai* in analogy to the *egeneto* of v. 3 and v. 6. Among other things and entities in the world, there are children of God. But whether we prefer "become" or "be," at all events this has to be a very special and extraordinary *genesthai*. What does it mean to become or to be something which by nature no one in the whole world, in the world that does not know the Word, can either become or be? For this reason, as Zahn rightly stresses,[101] we do not have *tekna theou egenonto* or *gegonasin*. As the *hosoi* are not the subject of this central clause, the emphasis does not fall on the fact that they are or do this or that, but on the fact that the Word gave them the possibility of being something, the children of God, and of doing what is in keeping with this, receiving the Word and believing in his name. For an understanding of the whole we cannot emphasize too strongly this *edōken autois exousian*.

Thus far I have translated *exousia* very generally as "possibility." I now want to say more precisely, not possibility in the sense of *dynamis*. power, might, strength, but in the sense of *axiōsis*. authority, legitimation, right. It seems to be an offense against the divine order, according to which darkness can never be called light, that there should be those living within the world who can boast that they are called and are God's children. How does this come about? They have to be authorized, legitimated, given a right to be able to do this. Without the corresponding *exousia* no one can be a child of God. Nor can any take this *exousia* to themselves. They must be given it. We think of the opening clause of 1 John 3:1: *idete potapēn agapēn dedōken hēmin ho patēr*, that we. . . . But we are not told here that the Father gives them the necessary *exousia*, nor, as Paul, and Calvin after him, might have said, that they are given it by the Holy Spirit, but rather (not contradicting

---

[101]Zahn, op. cit., p. 73.

these statements but giving them an unheard-of concentration) that the Word gave it to them. We do not deviate from the text if we recall that in the prologue to John the Word is a locum tenens for the one who later in the Gospel will be called especially "the Son." He gives *this exousia* who himself originally has it. The Word has it, for the Word is the Son, the firstborn of all God's children from all eternity. "He is born as alone the Son, and he did not want to remain alone. . . . This one who is alone the Son, whom God begot and by whom he created all things, he sent into this world so that he should not be alone but have many brethren."[102] The right of the *hosoi* to be children of God is thus enclosed and grounded in the Son. In this light we can understand John's hesitation to say *huioi* instead of *tekna*. Paul did not feel this because in him *huios* is less prominent as a term for Christ, although this does not mean that in his view the relation between Christ and his own is different. But let us consider what it means that it is the Word that gives the *hosoi* that *exousia*. If the children of God are the *lambanontes* or later the *pisteuontes*, and if it is the Word that gives them the right to be God's children, this obviously means that the Word himself is the authority by which the *lambanontes* and *pisteuontes* are what they have to be as such. As the Word is spoken to them, they are addressed and called. The Word gives them a new essential character, his own character. Their action becomes a grasping of the Word, their attitude a Yes to it. Their *exousia* to be God's children lies in this gift, this self-giving of the Word. They are oriented to it. We see then that the Word creates its own hearers. It is not at all that they are already there as *lambanontes* and *pisteuontes*, and for this reason can become God's children. They are *not* there! *Skotia* is there and not the *exousia* for this existence. The cosmos is there, *anthrōpoi* are there, *unfaithful idioi*, who do not understand themselves as such, are there. Into this non-being the light comes — Let there be light, and there was light [Gen. 1:3]! — the *exousia*, the right, to be children of God. "*Incredibilis rerum conversio tunc facta est, quum Christus excitavit ex lapidibus Deo filios.*"[103] Can one fail to see that revelation is presented

---

[102]Augustine, op. cit., II, 13 (p. 28) [see Eng. tr. p. 17]: For "many brethren" the text has "brethren raised up to the status of children."

[103]Calvin, op. cit., col. 11. [See Eng. tr. p. 17: "For this was an incredible change — that Christ raised up children to God out of stones."]

here as a self-enclosed circle into which no one can leap from outside? There are in the world *hosoi* who receive the Word. John
starts with this fact, which is just as axiomatic for him as the
givenness of the Word, which, now that he has heard the Word, is
identical with the fact of his own existence. But, he continues, the
fact that *in* the world they are not *of* the world, that they are God's
children, that their *lambanein* and *pisteuein* are not a great illusion
but an expression of the reality, that God's Word comes to them,
that they belong to God as children do to their father — all this is
per se theirs no more than it is anyone else's. The possibility of it
is given solely by the Word itself. *The Word* convinces, converts,
forces, and decides. The Word is subject and not object in this
action. *Gratitude* is the last and deepest thing with which such
people can grasp their existence.

  Their existence as believers; this is the point of the participial
clause at the end of v. 12: *tois pisteuousin eis to onoma autou.* For
scholars who regard the prologue as John's revision of an ancient
Christian original, it is tempting to claim that this final clause is
a Johannine gloss. It does indeed sound like a commentary, logically
if not grammatically related to the main clause like the nominative
absolute at the beginning. If it is a gloss — I will not discuss any
further this purely literary hypothesis — we have even more right
than if it is not, to regard it as an authentic interpretation of what
the author at the beginning of the verse was depicting with his
elabon auton as the action of the children of God. They, these
hosoi, were believers in his name. What does this mean? In a very
worthy excursus on believing and knowing, W. Bauer (op. cit.,
pp. 99f.) succinctly defines what John means by *pisteuein: pisteuein* is "regarding the church's confession of Christ as true." We
shall perhaps reach our goal most quickly by taking issue with this
definition. W. Bauer is certainly right when he points out that in
John *pisteuein* almost always has reference to Christ. The other
parts of his definition are in my view less on the mark. It must be
admitted that "the church's confession" is a rather arbitrary expression. The verb *homologein* occurs a few times in John and often
with the same objects as *pisteuein* has elsewhere. But *homologia*
itself as an object of *pisteuein* is a term alien to John. Similarly,
"church," *ekklēsia,* occurs only in a few insignificant passages in
3 John [vv. 6, 9f.]. The object of faith in John is neither what the
hosoi confess about Christ nor what they confess in concert as the

church. The only object calling for consideration is that as which Christ reveals himself or is known. W. Bauer has collected the various relevant definitions; there is belief in Christ as the Son, the Holy One of God, the light, and the resurrection and the life, in his heavenly origin and mission, in his relationship with the Father, in his all-decisive significance. But W. Bauer also refers to passages in which *pisteuein* is believing in Christ but remarkably without material definition, e.g., passages which on the one side speak about believing *eis auton* (2:11; 7:5; 12:11, 46), and on the other side those, to which the present passage belongs, where it is a matter of believing *eis to onoma autou* (2:23; 3:18; 1 John 5:13), and in the last two of the references the name "Son" cannot be meant, for they speak expressly about believing in the name of the Son. Analogously one may assume that the name in the present passage is not the name Logos but the name of him who is provisionally called the Logos but who later in the Gospel reveals himself as the Son, the Holy One, the light, etc., and who is known as such and is to be believed in as such.

But what does it mean that John simply speaks about believing in him or in his name? I first ask whether it is not necessary to rank this believing logically above the other (i.e., above explicit believing with a defined content). *Autos* or *onoma autou* obviously does not coincide exclusively with any one of the definitions but also does not exclude any one of them. It is as it were the common denominator or the subject of all the predicates. In the sense of John one has perhaps to assume that concretely one can believe only *eis auton* or *eis to onoma autou* when believing him as the Son, the Holy One, or with some other precise definition. One believes him as all these things as and because one believes in him himself or in his name. *Onoma* can mean three things here. (1) With H. Holtzmann, it can be "the sum of all the characteristic qualities that go with the holder of the name (the Logos or Jesus),"[104] i.e., the totality of what is otherwise defined as Son, Holy One, light, etc. (2) It can be very simply the human name Jesus, which in the Gospel itself becomes the dominant subject in place of the Logos. (3) It can be the ineffable name of Rev. 19, i.e., the reality in which all the qualities are united and which bears the human name Jesus.

---

[104]H. J. Holtzmann, op. cit., p. 41.

All three possibilities can at once be equated not only with the
autos but also with one another. All three ring out when the *eis to
onoma* is sounded forth in John, and nothing other than *autos* is
meant with this personalistically oriented formula taken from the
Old Testament. We may thus venture the thesis that in John believing is primarily *pisteuein eis auton* or *eis to onoma autou*. This
explains why here, where the term *pisteuein* occurs for the first
time, John uses *eis to onoma autou* after having already made rich
use of *autos* as the object of *egnō, parelabon,* and *elabon* in
vv. 12-13. Regarding Bauer's definition we may thus observe further that one might speak only about a confession *of* Christ, not
confession concerning him. Or, if we drop that formula, one should
not speak about knowledge or revelation concerning Christ, as
though the essential object of faith were what is revealed or known
about him and not he *himself* who, even if with precise definitions,
reveals himself and makes himself known. At issue is the revelation
and knowledge of Christ himself. The person reveals himself and
makes himself known, as we might also say paraphrasing the *autos*
or *to onoma autou*. Belief is in Christ himself, in his person. As a
divine person, we must add. The *autos* is the divine He, the *onoma
autou* is a divine, *the* divine, name. Divine in the strict sense of
vv. 1-2, not *like* God, but *equal* to God; the name of that person
who is another person distinct from *ho theos* and yet who is co-
essential with *ho theos* as himself *theos*. As and to the extent that
one believes in this person, one believes his deity. What would
believing "in his name," i.e., in this person, mean if this were not
at issue?

We may agree unconditionally with the last part of Bauer's
definition in which believing in John is said to be regarding as true.
Those who take immediate offense at this definition as intellectu-
alistic are on shaky ground.[105] For in John's Gospel, so far as I can
see, among almost a hundred instances there is only one (14:1) in
which *pisteuein* might denote the Reformation *fiducia,* which for
suspect reasons has become so beloved in more recent theology,
and even here the matter is by no means certain. Whether its object
is the sonship of Jesus, or one of the other definitions, or, as here,
primarily his name, i.e., Jesus himself, *pisteuein* is the attitude

---

[105]A: "Those who, following Herrmann, take immediate offense at this
definition will have hard going in John."

which both begins with *ginōskein* and leads to *ginōskein*, and in which one accepts, or regards as true, the absolutely supreme claim, the divine revelatory character, or, in brief, the deity of the person who bears that name. The emotion or intensity with which one does so plays no material role. Materially it is simply a question of affirming v. 2: *houtos ēn en archē pros ton theon*. He speaks and acts with me as God. This is certainly true.[106] Regarding it as true is not just an intellectual matter. How[107] can one accept a person as God except as a person? How can one regard God as true in this person except as one exists oneself? But the power of faith derives, not from its existential nature, but from its object. In faith it is a matter of the truth which gives itself, and expects, to be recognized and acknowledged by us. But the truth is the divinity of the name that the Evangelist proclaims. For this reason, objectively, he simply describes faith as the acknowledgment of this divinity, as the regarding of it as true.[108]

A word about the relation of this final clause to the two that precede it. We have said already that it is logically parallel to the first. If we keep in view the material connection between *lambanein, ginōskein*, and *pisteuein*, then we can say with H. Holtzmann and W. Bauer[109] that the present participle *pisteuontes* represents the consequence of the *elabon* for the *hosoi*, the habitual situation into which they have entered with their acceptance of the Word. I would rather say that *pisteuontes* (which does in fact describe a *habitus*) is one side of the matter that is present in and with the event of *elabon*. The other side of the matter is to be expressed in some way with a reference to *ginōskein*. It is left out here except

---

[106]Cf. the closing sentence of Luther's exposition of the Creed in his Shorter Catechism.

[107]A: "very true. There is no real need to be afraid of a purely intellectual believing. How."

[108]A: "as one exists oneself, existentially? The much feared mere operation of the understanding is something that is impossible in itself. No one has ever really managed it. It cannot be a danger. There is thus no reason to be forced by it into a more emotional, or a more sentimental and moral, definition of the concept of faith, to be forced away by it from the fact that faith is primarily a matter of the truth which expects, affirmed by us, to be acknowledged as the truth. John knows of no other truth than the deity of the name which he proclaims. For this reason he describes believing, coldly and soberly perhaps, but perhaps also very objectively, as the acknowledgment of this divinity."

[109]H. J. Holtzmann, op. cit., p. 41; W. Bauer, op. cit., p. 19.

as it finds implicit expression in the relation of *elabon* to *egnō* in
v. 10. It can be left out because the author's whole concern is to
establish the *genesthai* or presence within the world of those who
receive the Word. This is why the emphasis falls on the habitual
pisteuein. We must seriously oppose Holtzmann and Bauer, and
also Zahn, who agrees with them here, when they find in the last
clause the presupposition of the transfer (in the main clause) of
exousia to be God's children.[110] The text does not say this. Logically
the third clause is parallel to the second as well as the first. As in
Rom. 8:14, one can speak only of a coincidence or personal union;
those who believe in his name are the same as those to whom the
Word gave *exousia* to be God's children. Similarly in Rom. 8:14
the *agomenoi pneumati* are the *huioi theou.* It is not because they
are *agomenoi* or *pisteuontes* that they are *huioi* or *tekna theou.*
Indirectly we have to say the same about *pisteuontes* as about
elabon, namely, that with the *edōken* of the main clause the presupposition of *pisteuein,* too, is stated. To that extent what the
author wanted to say in both clauses emerges incontestably in the
continuation in v. 13. It is not what the *hosoi* are or do, but what
is done for them in their relation to the Word. Their right to be
God's children is absolutely given to them. They are miraculously
born, as v. 13 adds. Can this gift have its presupposition in what
they do, in their *lambanein* and *pisteuein,* and not the reverse?

   In linking v. 13 directly to v. 12 we answer already a textual
question that arises regarding v. 13. Tertullian (*De carne Christi*
19.24) bears witness to a text which began with *ouk ex haimatōn*
and ended with the singular *egennēthē,* and he argues against another text which began with *ouk . . .* but, like that acknowledged
today, ended with *egennēthēsan.* Tertullian argues against this text
as a Valentinian falsification.[111] A number of other western fathers
refer to the content of this verse in such a way that if the references
are more than allusions, i.e., quotations, they may undeniably be
claimed as further witnesses to the existence of a text that ends
with the singular *egennēthē.* Among the textual witnesses proper
the Latin Codex b has the reading *qui . . . natus est,* which seems
to point back to a Greek *hos . . . egennēthē.* On the other hand the
Cureton Syriac and the tradition that follows it stubbornly have

---

[110]Holtzmann and Bauer, loc. cit.; Zahn, op. cit., p. 75.
    [111]Quoted in Bauer, op. cit., p. 20, from whom the other references are also
taken.

the grammatically and logically impossible reading *hoi . . . egennēthē*. If this *hoi* and the ambivalent *qui* are to be erased as an
addition of the later Greek text, and if the reading of Tertullian is
to be accepted as original, then the verse goes with what follows
and not with what precedes. Zahn, who vigorously supports this
view, and who sets out the textual data in a valuable excursus,
stresses the *kai* with which v. 14 opens and which after the analogy
of the nine preceding instances of *kai* in the prologue forms a connecting link. He also finds that the verse is trivial, superfluous,
verbose, and unnecessary if it goes with what precedes.[112] On this
reading the content of v. 13 is not a statement about the *pisteuontes*
or *tekna tou theou* of v. 12 but a statement about the one of whom
it will afterward be said that as *ho logos* he became *sarx*. The
reference will then be to his being conceived or born — *gennasthai*
can finally mean both — not in the natural way but directly of God.
On this view the most natural understanding is that we have a
parallel here to the accounts of the virgin birth of Christ in Matt.
1:18ff. and Luke 1:26ff. This original statement of the text was
then changed by the Valentinians about A.D. 140 in the interests
of their special doctrine of the chosen race of spiritual men, and
through the Alexandrians Clement and Origen the reading *egennēthēsan* became the common catholic legacy and penetrated into
the west, although not without the interpolation of *hoi*, i.e., the
direct referring of *egennēthēsan* to *pisteuontes* (v. 12), in an attempt to remove any possibility of that special aristocratic and
esoteric interpretation of the Valentinians. Blass, Loisy,[113] and
R. Seeberg,[114] as well as Zahn, have opted for Tertullian's *egennēthē*. Against it the following arguments may be brought.
(1) Tertullian's complaint against the Valentinians has little plau-
sibility. What readers of the text that Tertullian calls falsified would
not have related *egennēthēsan* to the preceding *pisteuontes* with or
without a *hoi*? But this at once frustrates the purpose of the falsification. (2) The passages in the fathers adduced by Zahn in which
reference is made to Christ in the singular in verbal echoes of the
verse need not be quotations (with one important exception). They
may just be free allusions. In the light of the virgin birth it is natural

[112]Zahn, op. cit., p. 78.
[113]For Blass and Loisy, see Holtzmann, op. cit., p. 42.
[114]For Seeberg, see Bauer, op. cit., p. 20.

to speak of Christ in the phrases of this verse without thinking that this is its real meaning. (3) Except for b the Codices all agree on *hoi . . . egennēthēsan.* (4) The very argument that makes the isolated reading *egennēthē* or *natus est* probable — the dogmatic weight and fruitfulness of the reading — also makes its almost universal disappearance hard to understand. Would the Alexandrians, and later the whole east and west, have abandoned a testimony to Christ's virgin birth so easily, and without noticing the heretical origin of the plural? (5)[115] Is it likely that the Evangelist would suddenly take up here a theme that is really alien to the context and then let it drop again, not only in the prologue but also in the Gospel? All the things that we have heard thus far and are still to hear in the prologue are richly related both among themselves and to the remaining content of the Gospel. They form a well-ordered whole, and in central points are a little anticipation of the whole book. What is the point of the sudden assertion here of a definition of the appearance of Christ which the author certainly knew and accepted in some form but which, along with many another definition, he obviously had no thought of bringing in to build up his portrait of Christ?

If we regard these counterarguments as stronger and are thus satisfied with the usual text, then, as we have assumed, the verse stands in direct connection with v. 12. As a third and again a grammatically odd parallel, further defining the *autois* of the main clause of v. 12 along with the nominative absolute of the first clause and the participle of the third clause, we have the relative clause *hoi . . . egennēthēsan.* Strictly speaking, this is not saying anything new. But it is not on that account trivial or unnecessary. V. 2 says nothing new in relation to v. 1, and v. 11 says nothing new in relation to v. 10, yet Zahn does not find them trivial or unnecessary. V. 13 underlines analytically what is meant by *tekna theou.* The children of God exist exclusively from God. They are so related to

---

[115]A makes this point 6, and inserts as 5: "If we presuppose *egennēthē.* the relating of the three definitions with *ouk. oude. oude* to the virgin birth is the most natural one but it suffers from the serious difficulty that in view of the *ex haimatōn* it says much more than the virgin birth, ruling out all human cooperation. On the reading *egennēthēsan* this is not surprising, but it is very surprising if the aim is to describe the birth which in Matt. 1 and Luke 1 is one without a father but not without a mother."

God that in a way that is new compared to the whole cosmos and all other being, they are there through God, and indeed directly through God, or from God, so that in addition to the being that they have in common with all other being in the cosmos, transcending this previous being, they have a new being which is distinct from the being of the cosmos and cannot be derived in any sense from it. Materially, then, the *hoi* undoubtedly relates to the *tekna theou* but grammatically it relates to the *tois pisteuousin* or the *hosoi elabon*, although according to 2 John 1 taking *hoi* with *tekna* is not grammatically impossible. If in relation to v. 12 we finally rejected the view that *lambanein* and *pisteuein* are the presupposition of *edōken*, we now read that the *lambanontes* and *pisteuontes* have their origin in God, that they are really God's children. That misunderstanding of v. 12, which Zahn unfortunately accepts,[116] shows that v. 13 with its *hoi . . . egennēthēsan* is very much needed against the opinion of Zahn. No, says John, in opposition to this possible misunderstanding. What the Word gives, the *exousia* that the *lambanontes* and *pisteuontes* receive, relates to what God does or has done to them. As the proclamation of a right it issues from existent divine power and its exercise. The Word summons them to be what they already are from God and to do what they must do as those that they are from God. This summons, then, signifies a pure gift comparable to the Word of the Creator: Let there be light [Gen. 1:3] where there was no light, for its content (Be God's children) is saying what only God can say, and what, when he says it, already necessarily is, as he demands and promises, and is so from all eternity before those addressed have heard it, in principle before they receive and believe it, even though it is only as such, with the receiving of *exousia*, that they realized and recognized this being.

V. 13, like v. 11, is a little comparison, except, of course, for the "of God." It is rich in words so as to present the picture. Its point is that those who receive and believe in v. 12 confront their own existence as such as a miracle, a creation of God, from their own standpoint a new birth, the beginning of a new existence. The truth of their own existence, which has been initiated for them by the Word which per se convinces, converts, and compels, is a mir-

---

[116]Zahn, op. cit., p. 74.

acle, a creation, a new birth. It is so in relation to the existence of
the cosmos that is covered by darkness, to their own existence
insofar as it belongs to this cosmos. In no way can they know that
they are established and exist as receivers and believers except of
God. The comparison in v. 13 represents the negative way suggested by the expression "in no way." Sexual propagation is a type
of other kinds of establishment that are proper to the being of the
cosmos and to being in the cosmos. It is a type of the opposite of
miracle, creation, and new birth.

The plural *haimata* is odd. On the analogy of *sarkes* in Rev.
17:16; 19:18; and James 5:3, it might mean "matter (of the blood)
as the sum of its parts" (Holtzmann)[117] or *"longa generis successio"*
(Calvin).[118] Augustine[119] and Zahn[120] relate the remarkable plural
to the blood of the father who begets and the mother who bears.
If they are right and every analogy to natural birth is ruled out, not
excepting the virgin birth of Jesus Christ, then the existence of
believers as children of God is described as an even greater miracle
here than the virgin birth of Jesus Christ. If it is unlikely that this
is the author's purpose, then we have to choose between Holtzmann
and Calvin. For my part I prefer to stay with a *non liquet. Ek
thelēmatos sarkos* certainly denotes the impulse, or the instinct, or
the voice of human nature which impersonally but imperiously, yet
carnally, expressly characterized as earthly, unavoidably defined by
sin, is the true subject of natural propagation. *Ek thelēmatos andros* is finally and very realistically the decisive will and act of the
male. We have to think here especially of the aesthetic and religious
transfiguration and glorification with which that age more emphatically than many others surrounded the whole sexual sphere
and particularly the action of the male. We have also to think of
the obvious affinity between sexual generation and genius of all
kinds which in all ages has been felt and manifested with shame
or triumph. Only thus can we get the force of the comparison here.
Everything that points in this direction is meant to be stated, everything that is more closely or more remotely connected with it, every-

---

[117]Holtzmann, op. cit., p. 42.
[118]Calvin, op. cit., col. 12. [See Eng. tr. p. 18: "the long succession of the
line."]
[119]Augustine, op. cit., II. 14 (p. 29). [See Eng. tr. pp. 17f.]
[120]Zahn, op. cit., p. 79.

thing that can be more or less clearly understood in this way (and within the human realm what does not point in this direction, what is not connected with it, what cannot be understood in this way?).

None of this must be confused with the basis of the existence of the *hosoi* of v. 12 as this is created and given by the Word. These are born *ek theou* as no one and nothing else is born, as is possible only *ek theou.* "Here you must put away from your eyes all that is high, great, and glorious to the world, you must forget all creatures, for although all these things have their origin and beginning from God, through none of them can one become God's child. . . . The only thing is to be born of God, or else all is lost. . . . Everyone must creep into the gospel and become new there, putting off the old skin as the serpent does when its skin becomes old. . . . And thus one becomes a wholly different and new person who sees all things differently from before, who assesses differently, judges differently, thinks differently, wills differently, speaks differently, loves differently, desires differently, works differently, and then goes forward."[121] This is the last and supreme thing that John has to say about the work of the Word in its *erchesthai eis ton kosmon* in v. 9; with the authority that only God can have it presents to us the completed fact that we are of God and only of God. It sweeps all other foundations from under our feet and sets us on this one alone. It robs us of all the security of self-contemplation that does not consist of seeing ourselves as put in our place by God. It gives the *exousia* to burn all our ships behind us, to raise no more claim to genius, to know that we are secure on the far side of every natural self-understanding. It is thus that in the world the Word triumphs so greatly over the world that does not know it. It is thus that the light shines in the darkness and in defiance of the darkness that does not comprehend it. For where is the darkness where the children of God are? It is thus that the witness to the light in the world, the witness of John which is so important to the author, the other John, is not in vain.

14. **Kai ho logos sarx egeneto kai eskēnōsen en hēmin, kai etheasametha tēn doxan autou, doxan hōs monogenous para patros, plērēs charitos kai alētheias.** Zahn has laid emphasis on the fact

---

[121]Cf. Luther, WA 10, 1, pp. 233f.; taken from Eberle, pp. 89ff. [Cf. the English translation by J. G. Kuntsmann and S. P. Hebart, *Sermons.* vol. II, Luther's Works, vol. 52, ed. H. J. Hillerbrand (Philadelphia, 1974), p. 79.]

that nine times in vv. 1-13 *kai* has the significance of forming a
direct link between two separate statements.[122] This is correct. But
incorrect, it seems to me, is his conclusion that this use of the
conjunction has to continue and that it applies necessarily in v. 14,
so that v. 14 is a direct continuation of v. 13. We can overlook the
fact that *kai* may simply be used for emphasis or underlining, for
this is less common in John than in Paul, and certainly is not in
question in this verse. Yet we may still say that precisely in John
there is a *kai* in larger letters which has a continuing rather than
a connecting function, which connects passage with passage rather
than sentence with sentence (cf. 1:19, 24; 2:1, 13; 7:1; 9:1). The
view that v. 14 is a new or second beginning of the basic thought
cannot be convincingly refuted with an appeal to *kai*. A formal
indication of the correctness of this view seems to me to lie in the
fact that here for the first time since v. 1 the term *ho logos* reappears. A further indication lies in the terms *monogenēs* and *ho
patēr,* which occur here, which appear again in v. 18, and which
thus seem to combine the last five verses of the prologue into a
material unity.

The content of the verse is naturally decisive. Presupposed in
what precedes, something completely new and different, although
also its presupposition, now comes on the scene and becomes the
center of attention: *ho logos sarx egeneto.* Let us sum up what we
have heard about *ho logos* thus far. We know that the Word is
thought and spoken where God himself is, at the beginning of all
things. We know that it has itself the essence and nature of God
and therefore autonomy and personhood. It is the creative Word
before all things, and it carries the redemption whose light illumines men even in their darkness, the light to which the Baptist
testifies, only testifies, but really testifies. Thus the revelation of
the Word, and in the revelation the Word itself, comes into the
world. Not known by the world, not accepted by those to whom it
originally applies, it is still mighty and victorious, it still creates its
own hearers and recipients, because it is this Word, God's Word.
Of this subject it is now said: *sarx egeneto.*

Let us begin with the *egeneto.* The verb *ginesthai* has thus
far encountered us three times. In v. 3 it refers to the coming into

---

[122]Zahn, op. cit., p. 75.

being or the existence of all created things. What applies to them now applies to him by whom they come into being and are. In v. 6 *egeneto* denotes the historical coming of the witness John. Alongside him on the same level there now comes the one to whom he bears witness. In v. 12 *genesthai* signifies the existence of those who receive the Word as God's children, an existence for which the Word itself gives *exousia*. Now he, the giver, obviously comes alongside them, the recipients. Thus the well-known paradox of the verse lies already in the *egeneto*. What the predicate seeks to say is proclaimed already in the copula. There takes place — and for John this is, of course, the point and explanation of all that precedes — something which from what precedes might least be expected. The divine, creative, redeeming, revealing Word, whose sovereign being and action vv. 1-13 depicted, has left his throne, comes down to the level where creatures are, where the witness is, where the called are, takes his place in their ranks, loses himself as it were among all that and those who might have been the objects of his action, and himself becomes an object. He, the Logos, is there as something or someone else is there. The platonic schema of idea and reality, of original and copy, which in a pinch we might have used so far, whose use it has perhaps been the author's purpose provisionally to suggest, falls to the ground in face of this unequivocally asserted existence of the eternal subject. There also falls to the ground, there yields, the idea that in everything thus far that schema might have only heuristic and not strict or final significance. If we wanted to use it here, we should have to do violence to the text. Quite apart from *sarx*, we should have to decide whether *ho logos* or *egeneto* is meant improperly, whether, in crying contradiction to all that precedes, *ho logos* is not relativized as *a* word whose *ginesthai* is not unheard-of, or *egeneto* idealized so as to denote only an apparent becoming and being as whose subject *ho logos* is possible. But the use of *egeneto* thus far gives us not the slightest cause for this. The paradox is harsh and clear: *ho logos egeneto*, the Word became, it was there. The concreteness, the contingency, the historical singularity of the eternal, absolute, divine Word is what is stated with this sentence, and to understand John we must not take away anything on either side. But if we refrain from doing so and try to follow John, we cross the boundaries of idealistic thinking, and both before and behind, in presuppositions and conclusions, we have to be clear what has happened.

Without discarding the *einai* of v. 1 and all its specific content, the Logos now adds the *ginesthai* with its express and different specific content. Idealism is right with its antithesis. We cannot truly set this aside. No one can gather into a single thought the definitions that in its view are antithetical. No one can state them in a single word. Even John cannot do this and does not do so. But for him and therefore for us there is the requirement to see them as the definitions of one and the same subject, to think of them in concert. In interpretation of the *egeneto* here as in vv. 3, 6, 12, one must not put the main accent on the idea of coming into being. One should note the parallels in 1 John 4:2 and 2 John 7, which speak of an *erchesthai* of Jesus Christ, not *eis sarka*. but *en sarki*. The paradox of the statement in v. 14 is not that he *came* into the world, for this was said already in v. 9, but that he came in this way, in the *flesh*. The stress lies on the coincidence of Word and flesh which John states to be the mode of the coming. The sign that equates *ho logos* and *sarx* is the *egeneto*, which already has something of the predicate *sarx* about it, which is not a neutral sign but a very eloquent one, incomparably more pregnant than the *erchesthai en sarki* of John's Epistles. We should not ask whether the *egeneto* denotes the birth of Christ or the descent of the Holy Spirit upon him as witnessed by the Baptist in v. 32. The *egeneto* signifies the epiphany, the concrete historical existence of the Word in all its breadth, just as the coming of the Baptist in v. 6 refers to his total appearance and not simply to the first moment of his activity.

Yet the text does not merely say *egeneto*. which is expressive enough. With unsurpassable sharpness it says: *sarx egeneto*. In the first place, the word *sarx*, often used with *haima*, simply denotes the vital animal nature. In John, if I am not mistaken, it occurs only once (17:2) in a context where the further neutral sense of "humanity" might be in place. In a series of verses in 6:51ff. the reference is to the flesh of Christ, i.e., to what, according to this verse, the Word also is or became in virtue of the *egeneto*. But these verses shed no light on what *sarx* means here. Instead, it is decided here what the term means in ch. 6. Finally, in a third series of passages (1:13; 3:6; 8:15), *sarx* is unmistakably human nature in its exclusively hostile opposition to God or the Spirit, in its inability to comprehend them. This meaning seems also to be present even in 6:63, where it is the flesh of Christ of which it is said: *ouk ōphelei*. One can hardly suppose that directly after the pregnant use in 1:13 *sarx* has here the first and neutral sense. We shall thus stay with the third series. *"Ostendere voluit, ad quam vilem et abiectam conditionem Dei Filius nostra causa ex coelestis suae gloriae celsitudine descenderit. Scriptura, quum de homine contemptim loquitur, carnem appellat. . . . Eo usque se Filius Dei submisit, ut carnem istam, tot miseriis obnoxiam, susciperet."*[123] Becoming flesh, *ensarkōsis,* is thus something much more precise than becoming man, *enanthrōpēsis,* although later the terms are used interchangeably, and the latter is certainly included in the former. That the Word became a man is not the primary issue. Nor is it the point that the Word assumed human nature in general, although this is also included. The parallels from religious history collected by W. Bauer — the taking of human form by Isis and Osiris and Aesculapius and the Mandean Anoš Uthra, the Mandean epiphany in John the Baptist or the epiphany in Buddha or Zoroaster[124] — these are not true parallels, for they implicitly refer only to becoming man. But John speaks explicitly of becoming flesh, of assuming the nature of Adam, of the servant form which is proper to human nature under the sign of the fall and in the sphere of darkness, of the fallen and corrupt human nature which needs to be sanctified and redeemed. Naturally this includes the assuming of human nature in general, the assuming of human substance as soul and body in the form of an individual, and this, of course, not abstractly but concretely in the form of a specific human individual. But this is not where the emphasis lies. It lies on the fact that it was the *"humilis misera ac infirma hominis conditio" (Leid. Syn. Disp.* XXV, 14)[125] to which the eternal Word gave itself. With the use of *sarx* one cannot *not* think of all that is said and hinted in v. 5 and then again in vv. 10-13 about the world's resistance and lack of receptivity to the Word. I will interject a few words to this effect from Hermann Bezzel, for whom this thought is of special importance: "The Word . . . did not just enter into the reality of humanity

---

[123]Calvin, op. cit., col. 13. [See Eng. tr. p. 20: "He wanted to show to what a low and abject state the Son of God descended from the height of His heavenly glory for our sake. When Scripture speaks of man derogatorily it calls him 'flesh'. . . . Yet the Son of God stooped so low as to take to Himself that flesh addicted to so many wretchednesses."]

[124]W. Bauer, op. cit., p. 21.

[125]*Synopsis Purioris Theologiae. Disputationibus quinquaginta duabus comprehensa* (Lugdunum Batavorum, 1642), pp. 297f.

as it was originally intended by God but into the full seriousness
of the corruption of the human image."[126] "He became flesh. Jesus'
becoming man would never have saved us, only his becoming flesh.
. . . His becoming man would simply have heightened our pain:
'Why could not you be such a man as he?' It would simply have
proved what we could have been if we had not fallen. His becoming
man would have been as it were a mocking of my plight" (p. 61).
But he "did not merely bear the body; he bore the body of weakness.
In virtue of the divine realism he did not merely choose for himself
the being of man; he chose for himself all the deep poverty of the
cosmic impotence and limitation of fleshly being." He "lived out
the idea of humanity in its distorted form" (p. 62). *Ho logos sarx
egeneto* means: *"pro immensa gratia ad sordidos et ignobiles se
aggregat Christus"* (Calvin, *Institutes* II, 13, 2) [see the English
translation by F. L. Battles, ed. J. T. McNeill (Philadelphia, 1960),
vol. I, p. 477: "Christ of his boundless grace joins himself to base
and ignoble men"]. The Logos puts himself at the side of his own
opponents. His relation to the world that inconceivably resists him,
his triumph in those who just as inconceivably receive him, is in-
adequately understood so long as the relation is seen only in terms
of antithesis or contrast. Vv. 12-13 rule this out already. *Ho logos
sarx egeneto* — the presupposition of all that precedes is now dis-
closed — means that the antithesis, the distance, the abstraction
that is created by the fact of darkness, of *ouk egnō* (v. 10), or *ouk
elabon* (v. 11) on the one side, and by the deity of the Logos on the
other, is overcome — how else would the point of vv. 12-13 be possible? — by a third inconceivable thing, namely, that the Word is
there as others are, in the midst of the darkness. If there is a shining
of light, a coming of light into the world, a witness to it; if there
can be a giving to real people, living in the world, of *exousia* to be
God's children; if there can be real people to receive and believe the
Word, it is because the Word is not just the divine Word, the Word
of the beginning, the superior Word, the epitome of creation and
redemption, but because as all these things the Word is also flesh,
as all these things the Word is also what we are, how we are, on
the way to us, accessible to us. For this reason his revelation of
life is no mere idea but reality and therewith the possibility of an

---

[126] J. Rupprecht, *Hermann Bezzel als Theologe* (Munich, 1925), p. 63.

action, of God's address to us. How could there be an address of
God to us had the Word not become man as we are? But how could
he have become man as we are had he not become flesh? God's
own Word in itself, as God thought and spoke it from his throne,
in the light that none can approach [1 Tim. 6:16], God's Word in
the concealment in which it was in the beginning, in which it was
with God and was God, God's Word in the form of an angel or
finally in the form of a man who by nature stands on the far side
of the darkness in which we ourselves stand—all this might be
God's Word but it would not be God's Word as his revelation of
life to us. As such it could be light in itself but it would not shine
for us or come as light into the real world. There could be no
witness to it. It could mediate no *exousia.* By definition it would
not be the object of human *lambanein* and *pisteuein.* That the Word
became *flesh* is its revelation. Because of another paradox that
meets the paradox of darkness on its own ground, we *do* have all
these things in principle: the glimmering, the brightening, and the
shining of the light during but also after and before his epiphany,
in all ages and places of the cosmos, for all that is called flesh. The
Word itself is *also* flesh. If, as in some modern exegesis, we adduce
the parallels in 1 John 4:1f. and 2 John 7 and say that this verse
shows an "antidocetic trend," this theory (which in my view cap-
tures the purpose of the Johannine writings very well in special
contrast to the Synoptics)[127] is only the historical expression of the
material train of thought which they develop. They combat Doce-
tism because they establish the reality and possibility of revelation
by a vigorous *en sarki.* In view of the theological importance of the
verse let us now attempt a more detailed evaluation. Three things
call for notice.

  1. I called the *egeneto* the sign equating *ho logos* and *sarx.*
By way of restriction, however, one must add that the equation
cannot be reversed. *Ho logos* must remain the subject and *sarx* the
predicate. The Logos is what he is even without this predicate. The
flesh exists in the concrete sense of the statement only as the predicate of the subject Logos. The Logos is the person that here is
man. Schlatter expresses this relation when he says: "A man arose
out of the Word. He was made by the Word. He was the construct

---

[127]A: "(which has less to be said for it in relation to the Gospel than the
Epistles)."

of the divine Word."[128] The dogmatic statement of the early church
is more cautious and refined: *ho logos assumpsit carnem.* W. Bauer
also talks about the taking of *sarx* by the Logos.[129] Certainly this
flesh arises only when the Word assumes it, when it becomes person in it. But it does not arise out of nothing, nor, as Schlatter puts
it, "out of the Word," but out of the total mass of human nature,
out of a particle of humanity, *"ex Maria virgine,"* as the later phrase
defines it more precisely. Yet one cannot emphasize too strongly
the *superiority* of the Word over the flesh that it assumes, which
is obviously Schlatter's concern. The *Word* speaks, the *Word* acts,
the *Word* reveals, the *Word* redeems. The *Word* is Jesus, the I that
will alone speak for long stretches later in the Gospel. Certainly
the *incarnate* Word. Hence not without the flesh but in the flesh,
through the flesh, as flesh. Yet the *Word!* One should not ignore
the sovereign emphasis that falls on this first member of the equation after all that has preceded. Otherwise one hopelessly destroys
what John is seeking to say.

2. It is "not the opinion of John that with the assumption of
sarx Christ ceases to be *ho logos.*"[130] The equation cannot cease
to be the equating of two unequal things, a paradox. No change
takes place, no transubstantiation, no replacing of the Word's mode
of being by another, no dissolution of the *logos* in *sarx,* and also
no development of a mixture of both, but a full union in which
nothing is taken away from the divine determination of the Logos
and nothing is added to the creaturely and sinful determination of
the *sarx.* He is now "very God and very man," not one or the other,
and not a third thing between them. In the words of Bengel: *"Idem
ille, qui antehac Verbum, qui Vita, qui Lux erat, idem Caro iam
factus est. Quod prius fuerat, id esse non desiit: at factus est, quod
non fuerat prius."*[131]

3. The meaning of the equation is the reality and possibility
of revelation, we said. The Word, however, is and remains the

---

[128]Cf. Schlatter, op. cit., p. 6.

[129]Cf. Bauer, op. cit., p. 21.

[130]Bauer, loc. cit.

[131]Bengel, *Gnomon* I, p. 562 n. [See Eng. tr. vol. II, p. 248 n. 1: "That same
Being, who was previously the Word, who was the Life, who was the Light, the
same was now made Flesh. What he had been before, that He did not cease to
be; but He was now made what He had not been before."]

subject of revelation. As it assumes flesh, flesh becomes the organ, instrument, or medium of revelation. But revelation is an event, an *action* of the Word. For this action the Word uses the *function* of flesh, but revelation does not become a state or quality or property of flesh. One may rightly say that flesh is sanctified when assumed by the Word. It is separated from all else that is flesh. But it is sanctified and separated for this function or ministry. We must indeed state that because the one who is person in it is a divine and absolutely sinless person, it may be called, with Paul in Rom. 8:3, the *homoiōma sarkos hamartias,* but not *sarx hamartias.* In ch. 6 there can be reference to the eating of this flesh by believers. In modern terms we can say that revelation is historical, and that only if it is historical is it possible and real. But from the sanctification of the flesh for service by the *ensarkōsis* of the Logos one may not conclude that the *sarx* itself is now revelatory in and of itself. One must not suppress the fact that in and of itself the flesh of Christ as *homoiōma sarkos hamartias* has neither after nor before any revelatory power or effect. One must not forget 6:63: *to pneuma estin to zōopoioun, hē sarx ouk ōphelei ouden.* One may not say that history itself is revelation. Nowhere and never is it this abstractly. The so-called historical Jesus, abstracted from the action of the Word, is *not* revelation. The revelatory power and effect of the predicate *sarx* stands or falls with the action of the subject *ho logos.* Revelation is nowhere and never the work of the *sarx* as such, not even of the *sarx* of Christ. It is totally the work of the Logos that has become *sarx. He* is the Jesus Christ who will authoritatively take up the word in the Gospel. If Jesus Christ does *not* do this work of his, the *sarx* can and must conceal, hide, and shut, even though it is the *sarx* of Christ. But just as certainly it can and must reveal when Jesus Christ *does* this work of his through it. No one has emphasized as much as the Fourth Evangelist that Christ can both reveal himself and not reveal himself. That the *sarx* is only *homoiōma sarkos hamartias* and not *sarx hamartias* is overlooked when Christ does not reveal himself. Part of the servant form which is assumed is that the divine person who is flesh here takes it upon himself and is pleased to let himself be numbered self-evidently among the transgressors [cf. Mark 15:28], to be seen as a companion of publicans and sinners [cf. Matt. 11:19], to be the reason for the most grievous offense. He can and must accept this when he becomes flesh. As flesh, if he *will* not reveal himself, he is *not* revealed but concealed and scandalous. His revelation cannot be known except with this danger of offense, since it can be known only in the flesh. Flesh would not be flesh without the full possibility of offense. For the Logos would not be the Logos if he did not have and exercise in the flesh the full freedom to give or to withhold. The *sarx* is a means of dialogue, of a dialogue in which there are pauses, not of a single unbroken note. If we want to say more, let us be careful that we do not say less!

We now turn to what follows: *kai eskēnōsen en hēmin.* Two interpretations call for notice, and the whole verse takes on a different aspect depending on the one we adopt. Since both have equally strong linguistic and material support, I am inclined to think that we have here deliberate ambivalence which can hardly be regarded as strange in view of the paradoxical character of the main statement of the verse. *Skēnē* or *skēnōma,* according to 2 Cor. 5:1, 4; 2 Pet. 1:13f., is first our perishable, earthly existence, our being as soul and body, understood as a transitory dwelling which, when it has served its turn, must be torn down as *epigeios oikia,* or put off like an old garment, to yield to the *oikodomē ek theou.* We need not speak here of the highly indirect identity of the two *oikiai* that undoubtedly emerges especially from Paul's doctrine of the resurrection (2 Cor. 5; cf. 1 Cor. 15). It is natural to suppose that the *ho logos sarx egeneto* is now taken to mean that when the Logos is among us, then, like us, he is tied to a dwelling which is destined to be destroyed. Heb. 11:9 points in this direction when it says significantly that Abraham, Isaac, and Jacob lived in tents as strangers in the land of promise, that they camped out, that they did not dwell in permanent houses, for *in* their country they were still *seeking* their country (11:14). This would give *skēnoun* here the significance of denoting the provisional, transitory, and episodic nature of the mode of being of the Logos indicated by *sarx.* It is hard to see why Zahn calls this interpretation "inappropriate."[132] Yet it is certainly not the only possible significance of the term. If John wanted to say only that the Logos was among us *temporarily,* the statement is surprisingly out of keeping with the verse as a whole. Let us quietly agree that *skēnoun* does denote the alien status to which the Logos gives himself by becoming flesh. What

---

[132]Zahn, op. cit., p. 81.

takes place when the Word becomes flesh *en hēmin,* among us, is a visit from "the dayspring from on high" (cf. the AV rendering of the *episkepsetai* of Luke 1:78). The rest of the verse demands, however, that we inquire further. The negation that the term includes must also have here some positive sense. And indeed we cannot fail to be reminded by the *skēnē* or *skēnōma* of the Old Testament tabernacle in which God takes up his dwelling "among men" (*en anthrōpois,* Ps. 78:60 LXX). What is said afterward about seeing the *doxa* of the Logos points us convincingly in the same direction. *Doxa,* the manifestation of God's glory, points to Hebrew *kabod,* power and dominion, but also to the fulness of light, the *shekinah,* which takes its name from its hovering or dwelling or enthroning between the cherubim above the ark of the covenant, and which constitutes the concept of the *skēnē,* of the tabernacle of God on earth. When John speaks immediately afterward about this *doxa,* we have to assume that in the *skēnoun* he was thinking very positively of God's solemn taking up of his dwelling among men in this way. On the other hand, we must not overlook the transitory aspect which is expressed in the term quite apart from its connection with *sarx,* which is indeed unavoidably stated also *precisely* in this recollection of the Old Testament *skēnē.* If in Heb. 9:9 this is a *parabolē eis ton kairon ton enestēkota,* and if the messianic present is the fulfilment of this *parabolē,* i.e., if it has brought the true and eternal tabernacle in Christ, the strict, universal, and definitive *skēnoun* of God *met' autōn* (Rev. 21:3) has still to come eschatologically. What is now called the *skēnoun* of the Logos *en hēmin* is indeed fulfilment in relation to Old Testament *skēnē,* but it is only promise, only the provisional and transitory *skēnoun* of a visit in comparison with the future *skēnoun.* The being of the Logos among us is — necessarily — both fulfilment and promise. If we think of fulfilment, the translation "to dwell" is better, but if we think of promise, the translation "tabernacle" is preferable. Perhaps better than both is "to lodge." The Logos has really lodged where we are, in this aeon. He has not just pitched his tent on the edge of our sphere of existence but taken up lodging in it. *This* is what is meant by *ho logos sarx egeneto.* But he has not come to dwell here, to be at home here. He has come to lodge and then go back again. The Logos has really come only for lodging. This, *too,* is what is meant by *ho logos sarx egeneto.* The incarnation of the Logos means that he has been among us — and in the present context everything depends on this positive side. But to define the positive side the negation is needed which is contained in the *skēnoun*: He has been with us *temporarily*. To be flesh means per se, for the Logos as well as for us, to be a *paroikos* or stranger, to have no permanent dwelling, *"ad tempus instar hospitis adesse."*[133] The nature of revelation in the flesh denotes its limit. It is the direct and complete revelation of God, but coming to us who live in the flesh it has this form. Its other form, which coincides with the resurrection of the flesh, still awaits us. Here and now it has to have this form. Only as revelation in the flesh that is not yet redeemed, and therefore only as transitory, once-for-all revelation, can it be real revelation here and now. The divine *skēnoun* without this negative definition of its positive side, the *skēnoun* whose nature does *not* also denote its limit, does not come under faith; it comes under sight and therefore under hope.

Who are the "we" of the *en hēmin*? Not the same as the ensuing "we" of the *etheasametha,* who apparently form a smaller and more specific circle. The Logos came even to those who did not perceive him. He was there where Caiaphas and Pontius Pilate and Judas were. They saw his *sarx,* they saw his *skēnoun.* They perhaps even saw something "glorious." But they did not perceive him. They did not *know* what they saw. It was as if they had seen something else. The glory of the *Logos* was *hidden* from them. It had to be, for it manifested itself in the flesh. With some it was different. They perceived. Thus the statement *eskēnōsen en hēmin* does not lead us beyond the *ho logos sarx egeneto.* It paraphrases and analyzes. This is what took place with the incarnation of the Word. The Word was among us; it was where we are, in time. There is a place in time where its *skēnē* was erected, where he put up, where he found lodging. He came out of the eternal world into this aeon, as transitory as everything else in this aeon, but also as concrete and objective as everything else. To reveal himself, he had to be concrete and contingent and perishable. He *was.* The apostolic witness is that he was. Because the *Logos* became flesh, the witness is worthwhile and divinely *necessary.* Because the Logos became *flesh* the witness is possible and has an object. On this

---

[133]Calvin, op. cit., col. 15. [See Eng. tr. p. 21: "He stayed for a time, as a guest."]

ground it has also its *human* necessity. Those who know must tell those who do not who it was that lodged here.

What follows, *kai etheasametha tēn doxan autou*, cannot be said of all the contemporaries of the *ensarkōsis*. For we (in particular) perceived the glory of him who lodged among us (in general). If the first two statements name and define the object of witness, a brief summary of the witness comes with what now follows. "We perceived" – this is John's only term here for what constitutes the witness. It stresses that which, in contrast to merely seeing and hearing with the eyes and ears, as in the case of Caiaphas and Pilate, makes him an apostolic witness. Note the greater clarity which is achieved as compared to the parallels in 1 John 1:1f., where we have hearing, seeing, looking, and touching, and the repetition puts seeing and hearing strongly in the forefront, although not without obscuring to some extent what is meant by the special perceiving of the apostolic *hēmeis*. Here the matter is plain. Their special mark is that they can say: *etheasametha. Theasthai* can denote the type of seeing with which a play or the appearance of a prominent person affects one. Or it may denote seeing in which one grasps the significance of what is seen. Or finally, as a technical term, it signifies the vision of God in the mystery religions. Whichever of these senses predominates,[134] what is undoubtedly meant is seeing with an attentiveness and a result that mark off those who perceive from others who only see. Obviously we have in *etheasametha* the same apostolic plural as in 1 John 1:1-4. But we are not to take the word as historically as Zahn does, who finds a reference here to "the personal disciples of Jesus."[135] And I am even less inclined to find in this plural a plural of majesty (denoting the disciple John according to Zahn). The exalted personage in the prologue is the other John, John the Baptist, though the name covers the author as well as the Baptist. And if there is an "I" in the *etheasametha*, it is that of the one who directly afterward, as one of those who perceive, at the center of the circle of those who perceive, bears witness to what he has perceived, namely, the Baptist. Let us be content, then, to affirm that we have here a "we" of majesty in which the first generation, or whoever is authorized to speak for it, speaks to the generations that follow. In distinction

---

[134]A: "suggests itself."
[135]Zahn, op. cit., p. 82.

from the many among whom the Logos lodged, this "we" *perceived.*
What? Not the incarnate Logos as such. The others see the incarnate Logos, although without perceiving, without knowing what
they see. The text does not say (Augustine stresses this):[136] "the
glory of the Incarnate." The others see this, although without perceiving it, without being made apostolic witnesses by the glory that
was perhaps to be seen (the *doxa* that the image of Christ in history
or in art may seek to recapture). *This doxa,* the radiance of the
assumed *sarx,* of the earthly personality of Jesus, can be seen or
not seen, but apostolic perception does not depend on this and is
not identical with it. Those who know what they see when they see
the Incarnate, the one who lodges among us, perceive the *doxa
autou,* the glory of the Logos. He himself is manifest in the *homoiōma sarkos hamartias,* God's own Son (Rom. 8:3). The Logos
as such is the bearer of the divine *doxa.* This is *his* glory. Those
who perceive him in the flesh perceive therewith God's glory. The
continuation speaks of this.

Let us stop for a moment at the *doxa.* The different possibilities of meaning in the term, which derive from the Old Testament
and the language of the mysteries, all meet in the idea of light, of
perfect radiance, of total brightness, such as proceeds from God's
mighty working and ruling, or simply from his presence. *Doxa*
differs from *phōs* in vv. 4f., if I am right, in the fact that it does
not denote God's divine self-manifestation as such but the qualities
of God that are at work in it, or may be seen where he reveals
himself, being also and primarily proper to God as such. As the life
that is contained in the Logos reveals itself (v. 4), it is known as
the source and epitome of all divine revealing, as *alētheia,* as it will
later be called, and also as the source and epitome of the redeeming
life which is the material content of revelation, as the *charis* in
which God comes to the help of the imprisoned world. What is
thus perceived in the Word is its *doxa.* We have perceived this in
the flesh, says John. This statement proves that he does not really
think that with the Incarnation the Logos ceases in any way to be
totally what he is. No negation is meant by what Phil. 2:5ff. describes as his *kenōsis* and *tapeinōsis* (achieved by taking the form
of a servant). He is concealed and yet, to those who perceive, not

---

[136]Augustine, op. cit., II, 16 (p. 31). [See Eng. tr. p. 18.]

concealed, in the possession of perfect divine *doxa*. "*Dei maiestas non fuit exinanita, quamvis carne circumdata esset: latuit quidem sub carnis humilitate, sed ita tamen ut fulgorem suum emitteret.*"[137] *Etheasametha tēn doxan autou* thus means unquestionably that we perceived his *deity.* We saw the Word in the flesh, and the Word was God; it was the divine *doxa* that we perceived. Holtzmann and Bauer seem to assume that John thought of the penetration and manifestation of the deity through the husk of the *sarx* as a kind of unbroken and ongoing process.[138] But this would again make the revealing a quality, as it were, of the *sarx,* something that is self-evidently given always and everywhere in and with the *sarx.* It would not do justice to the verb *doxazein,* which is very common in John, and which indicates that John thinks of the penetration as an isolated, if common, event rather than a continuum, as a concrete happening which strikes like lightning. To think of visionary experiences and the like makes no sense, nor does it help to ask why in the Synoptics the *doxa* of Jesus is expressly seen only once before the Resurrection, namely, at the Transfiguration [Mark 9:2-13 and par.], whereas in John it is constantly taking place. To this question one can reply only that in John we have a consideration of the life of Jesus in principle and that this works with fixed categories which may be seen in the Synoptics only in the form of isolated attempts at interpretation, although one may not deduce from this that the portrait of Jesus which is attempted differs in the two cases.

The *autou* that follows *doxan* finds an explanation in the added *hōs monogenous para patros.* The *hōs* is not necessarily saying, as Holtzmann and Bauer assume,[139] that what follows is meant as a comparison or a figure of speech: as in human life an only son shares what belongs to his father. John has too strong a material interest in the Father-Son relation to make it credible that precisely here he is using it only as a comparison. When v. 32 says of the Holy Spirit: *katabainon hōs peristeran,* the *hōs* hardly means that we have no more than a comparison, and this is certainly not

---

[137]Calvin, op. cit., col. 15. [See Eng. tr. p. 21: "The majesty of God was not annihilated though clothed in flesh. It was indeed hidden under the lowliness of the flesh, yet so that it still sent forth its glory."]

[138]H. J. Holtzmann, op. cit., p. 44; W. Bauer, op. cit., p. 23.

[139]Holtzmann, op. cit., p. 45; Bauer, op. cit., p. 23.

the case when 12:35f. says of the walking of the disciples: *hōs to phōs echete* (cf. also 2 Cor. 5:20: *hōs tou theou parakalountos,* and Matt. 7:29: *hōs exousian echōn*). The absence of the article before *monogenous* is not important because *monogenous,* relating to *autou* and referring back to *ho logos,* can have the force of an adjective. If *para* as a preposition is never found elsewhere with *gennasthai,* if it is also not attested elsewhere with *monogenēs,* and if it does not seem possible, with Zahn,[140] to coordinate *para patros* syntactically with *monogenous,* the probability seems to be (Holtzmann, Bauer)[141] that it is put there expressly to make impossible a foolish misunderstanding of the relation of *monogenous* to *patros. Patros* thus becomes a simple genitive, and the whole addition, while formally belonging to *doxa,* has in fact the character of apposition to *autou:* "We perceived the glory, the glory of him who is the only Son of the Father." To be sure, the lack of an article before *patros* remains a difficulty, because nowhere else in the Gospel, not even in v. 18, is the article missing except in the vocative. Nevertheless, the meaning of the whole statement is clear. Here for the first time the Logos is to be called the Son of God. And the occasion is the reference to his *doxa.* i.e., to an attribute which can only be God's, which is indeed (Heitmüller) "the distinctive form of the existence and manifestation of God and his world, [. . .] the epitome of God's powers and qualities."[142] How does he come to be the bearer of *doxa?* What is this *doxa* of his that we have perceived in the flesh? Answer: It is the *doxa* that he bears with right and necessity as the *Son* of God. To suppose with Zahn that this is a special *doxa,* different from that of the Father, can only cause confusion.[143] The point of the addition is not to stress distinction but to stress what the Father and Son have in common. Hence we do not simply have *hōs huiou,* but, in a way that brings the Son very close to the Father, *hōs monogenous para patros.* He is the only-begotten of the Father, the Son of God absolutely in a unique and special way, not *a* but *the* Son of God. *Monogenēs,* used of one whose deity has emerged generally from what precedes, sets him alongside the one whose *monogenēs* he is.

---

[140]Zahn, op. cit., pp. 83f.
[141]Holtzmann, op. cit., p. 45; Bauer, op. cit., p. 23.
[142]Heitmüller, op. cit., p. 195.
[143]Cf. Zahn, op. cit., pp. 83f.

The addition is thus saying the same as v. 1c but it is now expressly naming the first person. This second person, the Logos, whom we have perceived in the flesh, is of the same substance as that first person, is himself *theos*. This is why he bears the *doxa*. This is why his bearing of the *doxa* proves his *deity*. John will make further use of this *monogenēs*. this strengthened term for sonship, e.g., just after in v. 18, and again in 3:16, 18 and 1 John 4:9. We may mention that the term, which is not without Mandean parallels, is also used of the Babylonian god Mumma, the Arabian Dusares, the Logos in the Hermetic writings, and finally the phoenix bird, and it probably derives from an Orphic milieu. Here again, then, our author makes unreflecting linguistic use of a familiar word. That it comes in very solemnly and emphatically both here and in v. 18 is unmistakable. Its purpose — cf. the reference to the children of God in v. 13 — is to make it clear beyond all dispute whose glory we have perceived, who has brought us knowledge of God (v. 18). But materially the addition is more an underlining of the thought than its development.

More important in this connection is the conclusion of the verse: *plērēs charitos kai alētheias. Plērēs* is an indeclinable adjective. Grammatically, then, the last part of the sentence might go with *patros,* with *monogenēs,* with *doxan,* with *autou,* or finally with *ho logos* as the subject of the whole statement. Older exegesis fancied the last possibility.[144] Everything from *kai eschēnōsen* on then becomes a parenthesis. Modern scholars usually relate *plērēs* to *autou.* so that he who is the Father's only-begotten is now further defined as full of grace and truth. To me an epexegetical relation to *monogenous* seems even better. As the only-begotten he is the one who is *plērēs charitos kai aletheias.* i.e., according to v. 16, he possesses the fulness, the perfection, the quintessence, the *plērōma* of grace and truth. *All.* and the *epitome* of all that God shows and gives us of himself is proper also to his only-begotten. *En autō katoikei pan to plērōma tēs theotētos* (Col. 2:9). To this extent, as *monogenēs.* he is the bearer of the divine *doxa,* and for this reason — now this question receives a definitive answer — we perceived in him the divine *doxa.* It is truly *his doxa.* legitimately and necessarily. In saying this we have already established that *charis kai*

---

[144]E.g., Cocceius, op. cit., p. 17.

alētheia are meant in some way to be a further material definition
of the term *doxa*. But what is the additional factor? Zahn and
Schlatter rightly insist that there has to be a reference to God's
"great grace and faithfulness" (*rab ḥesed we'emet*) in Exod. 34:6.[145]
Against this view Holtzmann and Bauer object that the LXX renders *ḥesed* by *eleos* and that *'emet* means "faithfulness," not
"truth."[146] But might there not still be a free reminiscence of this
locus classicus of the Old Testament? Indeed, in the light of v. 17,
does there not have to be? It is none other than Yahweh-Kyrios
himself, appearing to Moses in a cloud, who says there that God
is "of great grace and faithfulness," and he does so at the very
moment when Moses, with two stone tablets in his hands, is climb-
ing to the top of Sinai to receive the law. Can it be an accident that
in v. 17 the *charis kai alētheia* that come by Jesus Christ are set
over against the law that is given by Moses? If the reminiscence is
plain in v. 17, it is already present here too, and we should not let
the freedom of the expression lead us to a denial of it. The only
thing is that, since the reminiscence is indisputably free, expositors
may not refer back so definitely to Exod. 34 as Zahn does. Bauer
tries to find in *charis* the supernatural power of deity and in *alētheia* the knowledge of God that derives from God. Holtzmann sees
subordination: "The generous favor of God to which we owe possession of the truth."[147] We perhaps stay closest to the text if with
Meyer we in some sense relate *charis* to *zōē* or redemption and
alētheia to *phōs* or revelation (v. 4).[148] V. 4 said of the Word that
in him was life and this life was the light of men. What is more
natural than to think of these terms here where we are told expressly what was the content or fulness of the Word? Yet the terms
do not need to be identical. *Charis* and *alētheia* denote what lies
behind *zōē* and *phōs* in the sphere of *doxa* which is not the same
as that of the revelation of redemption, although the one may be
seen in the other as its basis within the deity, as that which God
has and is in himself quite apart from the actual manifestations in
which he gives himself to be known as such by us. Grace and truth
are not actually to be coordinated, then, but subordinated along

145Zahn, op. cit., p. 81; Schlatter, op. cit., p. 7.
146Holtzmann, op. cit., p. 45; Bauer, op. cit., p. 24.
147Bauer, op. cit., p. 25; Holtzmann, op. cit., p. 45.
148H. A. W. Meyer, op. cit., p. 74. [See Eng. tr. p. 65.]

the lines of v. 4 in a way that relates them as content and form.
The only thing is, however, that as distinct from Holtzmann and
in the light of v. 4 we are to regard *charis* as the content and
alētheia as the form. The divine will and the divine power which
lie behind the revelation of redemption, which may be seen in it,
which constitute its seriousness and efficacy, are together, not di-
vided between the concepts but common to both, the *doxa* of both,
charis as content and *alētheia* as form. We perceived eternal grace
and eternal truth in the Logos. Herein he showed himself to be the
monogenēs para patros. Herein he is the bearer of the divine *doxa.*
Our witness to him, in brief, is thus that we perceived his glory as
his own. For the glory, God's glory, was truly to be perceived in
him, the only-begotten of God. Grace and truth, the eternal source
and epitome of the revelation of redemption, were to be perceived
in him. We saw and knew what was to be seen in him. We perceived
it.

15. **Iōannēs martyrei peri autou kai kekragen legōn, houtos ēn
hon eipon; ho opisō mou erchomenos emprosthen mou gegonen, hoti
protos mou ēn.** A second time, and just as unexpectedly as in v. 6,
the Baptist, or, again tacitly, John, confronts us. Unexpectedly? Perhaps not, to the extent that the relation between the first and second
parts of the prologue is plain. If we understood vv. 6-8 correctly in
the context of the first part, John is there a witness to the light that
shines, to its coming into the world, to the glimmering and dawn
that precede the sunrise, to Advent. He is so, not for himself alone,
but for all that comes under the concept of witness, and hence for
the author of the Gospel too. Every word that is said about John
the Baptist, John the prophet, is said about John the Apostle as
well. The apostles, too, are *anthrōpoi apestalmenoi para theou,* but
they, too, are only witnesses *peri tou phōtos.* We said already about
vv. 6-8 that those who bear witness to the shining of the light, to
its coming into the world, bear witness to the light itself. Where
there is brightness in the atmosphere it reflects the rising sun,
however weakly. The presupposition of Advent is Christmas. And
so, strangely, we have to say that the presupposition of the prophet
is the apostle.[149] V. 14 speaks about the presupposition, about the
light itself, the sunrise, Christmas, the apostles. With the *ho logos*

---

[149]A adds here: "If he were not objectively an apostle, he could not be
subjectively a prophet."

sarx egeneto we have seen how far the revelation to which the witness refers is possible and actual, how far with the fact of the object of witness the witness itself receives its *ratio,* how far the one to whom the witness refers comes to the witness (and the witness to him) so that the witness can be a real and authentic witness. The Word became flesh; this is why there are words about the Word. The light shines directly; this is why it shines and can be seen indirectly as well. The witness is an apostle; this is why he can be a prophet. If prophecy, *martyria peri tou phōtos,* is always the subjective significance of the work of an apostle (note the *peri autou* in v. 15, after v. 14), the objective possibility and reality of this work are grounded in the fact that he can say about himself what we now hear said in vv. 15-18 in exposition of the *etheasametha* and on the basis of the *ho logos sarx egeneto.* No wonder, we must now say, that the Baptist appears for a second time in v. 15. No wonder that he must now be characterized in principle for a second time in terms of his position and role — even here the true story of the Baptist does not yet begin. If Bultmann's hypothesis is correct,[150] we have to say that it is no wonder that the author regards this gloss as necessary. If the Baptist truly stands there among the prophets, he has to stand here among the apostles too. If he is typical on the one side with his pointing finger, he has to be on the other side by showing what he has seen, because something is to be seen. If he stands there for the author of the Gospel demonstrating by means of him how he himself is to be regarded, he does so here, too, by showing why the author is to be regarded in this way. If he had to be mentioned there where it was simply a matter of asserting the presence of witness, he really has to be mentioned here where it is a matter of uncovering its source and origin. If there was a need there, even from the standpoint of ecclesiastical politics, in opposition to a sect of John, to mark off his position and role from that of the light that shines in the world, even more so there is a need here, where, now that *ho logos sarx egeneto.* he confronts Jesus Christ as man to man. Face to face with the incarnate Word, he must now say his word, his human word, about himself and his relation to that Word. Note the fact, which is by no means accidental in this regard, that vv. 6-8 speak

---

[150]On this hypothesis, see above p. 13 n. 3.

about him in the third person but now in v. 15 he himself speaks
out of his concrete historical situation. Note further that now
for the first time in the Gospel and for the only time in the prologue
someone is introduced as a speaker. Note the present tense *martyrei.* Face to face with readers and hearers of the Gospel the Baptist still has to say what he says. And note the urgency: *martyrei
kai kekragen legōn.* How emphatic that is. Someone has *spoken*
here. Why? Because God's Word has been spoken. This Word evokes
human words to testify to it, and they are there. *By whom* are they
spoken? By the Baptist, yes, but again, the text has it, by John.
V. 15 could not, of course, be spoken by the other John, for here
the Baptist speaks out of his concrete historical situation. But the
houtos ēn is there as a point of comparison, and as a result we also
have the unconditional subjection of the witness to the one to whom
he bears witness. And of vv. 16-18 we have to say at least that the
author has done nothing, absolutely nothing, to rule out the inference, which all ancient exegesis drew, that here, in this preeminent
Christian and apostolic confession, John the Baptist is speaking in
the name of the *hēmeis. What* does he speak about? About the fact
that in principle the witness is surpassed and put in the shade by
the one to whom he bears witness; about his dependence on the
latter; about the latter's priority and superiority; about his own
position as a recipient relative to him; about his gratitude; about
the sovereignty and uniqueness of the Son of God as the Revealer
of God. This is what vv. 15-18 say, even if, as the ancients widely
advise, we regard them wholly as the saying of the Baptist, or even
if we split them between the Baptist and the Evangelist. This is
what they speak about. Let us now consider them in detail.

Martyrei, in connection with which *kekragen,* too, has the
significance of a present tense, describes the witness of John, in
Calvin's words, as a *"continuus actus"*: *"Perpetuo vigere debet haec
doctrina, ac si vox Ioannis perpetuo auribus hominum insonaret."*[151]
On this view the witness, like the Revealer himself, speaks as a
present and contemporary figure to the readers and hearers. The
author calls upon him to give his witness as if he were alongside
him. His witness is to the incarnate Word, and it is thus to the
same object as the author's own apostolic witness. Hence the *mar-*

---

[151]J. Calvin, op. cit., col. 16. [See Eng. tr. p. 22: "This preaching must
continually flourish, as if John's voice were continually sounding in men's ears."]

tyrei denotes an *actus continuus*. *Peri autou* links the Baptist's witness directly to what precedes. No *kai* or *de* separates him and his witness from the "we," or puts him on another level, or denies him the *etheasametha*. No, in an eminent way he seems to be one of those who has a share in it. What follows is remarkable enough, for the Baptist first quotes himself when he says: "This was he, this was the one I meant when I said. . . ." Let us first take the quotation separately: *ho opisō mou erchomenos emprosthen mou gegonen*. This means that he who follows me ranks before me; he has surpassed or overtaken me; the one who was behind me on the way is now ahead. This saying points to a fact which the speaker recognized as already complete when he spoke. The *gegonen* shows this. But he makes a paradox of it. Those to whom he then spoke it could not know whom he meant by the *opisō mou erchomenos*, and even less what the overtaking of the Baptist by him signified. Before their eyes the Baptist was unconditionally first as the man who speaks the last word. He can neither be replaced nor emulated. He is necessarily there as a genuine prophet in the ears of those who hear him as such. We usually take the *opisō mou erchomenos* as meaning the one who is born and comes on the scene after me. But obviously if the ensuing *emprosthen mou gegonen* has any meaning, the idea of the subordination of this later one in dignity and authority is also present. We are also led to this by the observation that everywhere else in the Gospels this is the point of *akolouthein* or *poreuesthai* or *aperchesthai* or *erchesthai opisō autou*: *Sequi aliquem ducem, alicuius sector esse* (cf. *aperchesthai*, Mark 1:20; John 12:19; *erchesthai*, Matt. 4:19; 16:24; Mark 1:17; Luke 9:23; 14:27). The *opisō mou erchomenos* shows that the one to whom it refers is a follower or supporter or successor or offshoot of the Baptist. Whether this is the meaning here depends on whether the *erchesthai opisō autou*, in the passages in which it undoubtedly denotes discipleship, is indissolubly bound up with the idea of external following on a journey on which the teacher and master finds himself. This would not fit here, for the Baptist is not an itinerant prophet but has a fixed location on the Jordan where the people come to him. But is *erchesthai* wholly identical with *akolouthein* and *poreuesthai*, in which, in connection with *opisō autou*, discipleship is characterized by the idea of physical following? Is it the view of the Gospels that all who followed Jesus (in the sense of *erchesthai opisō autou*) actually went after him? Or is there a relative if not absolute separation in meaning between this and the discipleship which distinguishes the disciples from the people who sometimes go or even run after Jesus? It would certainly fit the picture which the sect of John seems to have had of the relation of Jesus to the Baptist, or, which is even more important, the impression that must have been temporarily made by the baptism of Jesus by John, if here and in the Synoptic parallels the description of Jesus as *opisō mou erchomenos* marked him as standing in the shadow of the Baptist not only in time but also materially, as being dependent upon him.

However that may be, Jesus' standing in the shadow, or his material subordination, includes, as we have said, the commonly stated fact that he comes later in time. It was thought to be ruled out that one who came after the Baptist should be *ischyroteros autou,* to use the parallel phrase in Matt. 3:11. But the Baptist says that he is this too, here in the words *emprosthen mou gegonen.* He is speaking about a specific person who, coming after him, by the general verdict had to be inferior to him. He says that he is superior. If in the Synoptics the statement does not have unconditionally the character of a prophecy — *ischyroteros mou estin,* and I am not *hikanos* to untie his shoelaces, we read in Matt. 3:11 — in the present passage John the Baptist quite unmistakably speaks about something which at the very moment when he speaks is already in force even though his hearers do not see it: *gegonen,* I am already overtaken, set aside; the appearance is already a mere appearance, it was never the truth; the fact that this person came after me never meant that I was before him in dignity and authority. I already stand in his shadow even if in your judgment he and all others stand in mine. The only point is that you should see this too, that I should show him to you, this specific person in face of whom no doubt can arise as to who is subordinate, even though the other is first and is the master and the Baptist. For this word of subjection, which finds exact material parallels in the Synoptic sayings of the Baptist, and then in the saying about the shoelaces in v. 27, a reason is then added: *hoti prōtos mou ēn.* If this is not meant to be a simple repetition of the *emprosthen mou gegonen,* which would be pointless, then, ascribed by the Baptist to the specific person who comes after him, it cannot denote again his higher historical rank. It is designed to explain how far the relationship of historical ranking is the reverse of what it seems to be. *"Sensus est Christum*

iure praelatum fuisse Ioanni, quia excellentior esset.[152] And the
reason lies in the insight that this specific person who comes after
John is stronger than he, and has overtaken him, because he precedes him essentially and absolutely. He does not just precede him
in history as an elder precedes a younger, or a greater a smaller, or
a master a student. This is true too, but with a reversal of appearances. The only way that we can put it is that he precedes him as
God precedes all else and all others in history, as he precedes history as such. "Wholly in the spirit of the prologue a result that can
be recounted in history (that of vv. 19-27) is motivated by an eternal
relation, and what comes about on earth is explained by pretem-
poral being."[153] Or, with a specific reference, "Jesus with his earthly
ministry comes after the Baptist, but in truth the Baptist comes
after Christ, and he is called to his prophetic office because (!)
Christ as the first was with the Father."[154] *Prōtos mou ēn* means
that although this one comes after me in history, although, as one
may add perhaps more sharply, he is baptized by me, although to
all appearances he is my offshoot, nevertheless, I am in no sense
commensurable with him, I am not really worthy to untie his laces,
between him and me there can be no thought of rivalry, alongside
him I do not come into account, I find myself under him, in a
subordination to him which finds practical historical expression in
a reversal of rank: *emprosthen mou gegonen.* for which there are
in principle no analogies except the one which is much more than
an analogy, the subordination of the creature to him *di˙ hou ta
panta egeneto* (v. 3), or of believers to him who gave them *exousia*
to be God's children (v. 13). So greatly, in this sense, is he who
comes after me before me. By him I am who I am. It is out of place,
then, to raise with some exegetes the question where the Baptist
might have found this term *prōtos autou.* whether from study of
the Old Testament, or Philo's doctrine of the Logos, or prophetic
illumination. The only answer we can give in the sense of the Evangelist is that what makes the prophet a prophet, a witness to the
light that comes into the world, is that he *has* the concept of the
prōtos autou, the divine Word which is superior to him from all

---

[152]Calvin, loc. cit. [See Eng. tr. p. 22: "But the meaning is that Christ was
justly preferred to John because He was more excellent."]

[153]Holtzmann, op. cit., p. 47.

[154]Schlatter, op. cit., p. 8.

eternity and which thus makes it possible for him to be a prophet from all eternity, and that for this reason, in distinction from his hearers, even in history or in time, and were he the last and greatest prophet, he cannot think of regarding himself as the bearer of the final Word even relatively or on earth. What makes the prophet a prophet is that he knows that even on earth and relatively he is surpassed from the very first by him who comes, by the rising sun itself. He is a true and not a false prophet because he knows, and strange though it may sound to his hearers he says, that he who comes after me is stronger than I, is before me. What makes him a prophet is that in the present, bringing to light a present fact, he prophesies of Christ.

We now turn to the setting of this statement in v. 15. The statement itself is not the *martyria* of the Baptist but the referring of this earlier statement to the Logos that became flesh. To what does the *eipon* point us? We shall find much the same statement in much the same setting, with only minor variations, in v. 30. Even when John and Jesus are brought together in narrative and not in principle, an *eipon* points back to another time when the statement was made. One is tempted to think of v. 27, when on the day before meeting Jesus John did in fact speak about the *opisō mou erchomenos.* But in v. 27 he does not say what we find in v. 15 and v. 30 but utters the saying about untying the shoelaces. And in the Synoptics, too, we look in vain for the setting of the statement quoted in v. 15 and v. 30. V. 27 and the corresponding sayings of the Baptist in the Synoptics offer exact material (but only material!) parallels to the first half of the statement, but there is no parallel to the basis given in v. 15 and v. 30: *hoti prōtos mou ēn.* We thus face two possibilities. Either the Evangelist drew this statement from a special source or recollection, or he himself reduced the epitome of the Baptist's declaration of subordination to this formula. There is no merit in trying to work out which is the more likely. What is certain is that the statement (including the basis) sums up excellently what the known sayings of the Baptist in v. 27 and the Synoptic parallels say about the one who comes after him, and that it also expresses in a very pregnant way what the Baptist must in fact have been saying, prior to his meeting with Jesus, in the position and role which the historical portrayal of the Fourth Evangelist assigns to him. Those who in this and other matters are concerned about the historical question should let themselves be directed and instructed by the consideration that the historical portrayal of this Evangelist — irrespective of his qualities as a narrator — is in fact quite simply the correct and indeed the only possible one.

We are still left with the main point of v. 15. The statement becomes witness *peri autou* only as the Baptist quotes it in saying: *houtos ēn hon eipon.* "*Quibus verbis intelligit sibi hoc ab initio fuisse propositum, ut Christus innotesceret.*"[155] As a genuine prophet he neither could nor would want to do anything but bear witness to him who is greater than he because he is before him. Since this greater now stands in front of him, he confirms the authenticity of his mission by at once recognizing and acknowledging him: *This* is he . . . ! His subordination ceases to be a readiness and becomes an act, an event. For the hearers and spectators — these are his concern — before their eyes and ears, he retreats with this *houtos ēn* before the one to whom it applies, he explains that his own preceding and Jesus' following is a mere appearance, he renounces before them all his own precedence: This one has the precedence. As he subordinates himself not merely inwardly — he has done it inwardly long since so far as he himself is concerned; for him the readiness was already the act, and what he now does is simply the consequence of this act — as he states his self-subordination, pointing to the coming one as one who is not just abstractly propounded but concretely present; as he does not simply state it but proclaims it (*kekragen legōn*), in this act he becomes what as a prophet he is potentially from the very first: a *witness.* One might also say that this is the objectivity of the witness, proving itself in exemplary fashion at the most decisive point. He knows that his service consists of pointing to the one who is greater than he. He recognizes him as present. He states and proclaims that he recognizes him, and recognizes him *as such.* In so doing he renders what he knows to be his service. He thus acquires an actual share in the light of that greater one. He also speaks for every age when that greater one speaks: *martyrei . . . hina pantes pisteusōsin di᾽ autou* (v. 7). Thus "John" stands at the beginning of this Gospel, and — not for nothing — at the beginning of all the Gospels, and therefore of all the New Testament, not at the end, but as the

---

[155]Calvin, op. cit., col. 16. [See Eng. tr. p. 22: "By these words he means that from the very first his purpose was to make Christ known."]

quintessence of the Old Testament, which with him moves over into the New Testament. Only out of the readiness of the prophet can one become an apostle. Thus the Bible arises, God's authoritative Word, as the *witness* to revelation. Thus it comes about that there are those who will sit on twelve thrones and judge the twelve tribes of Israel (Matt. 19:28). One might compare this *houtos ēn* to crossing a mountain pass. As the Baptist says it, he is both prophet *and* apostle, a witness to both promise *and* fulfilment. Recognizing, in saying it, that the coming one is present, he participates in the *etheasametha* as he says it (v. 14). What else could he have said? The *prōtos mou* whom he recognizes, and behind or under whom he thus sets himself, is none other than the *monogenēs,* the bearer of *doxa,* the Logos who has come into the concealment of the flesh, the Word that was in the beginning, that was with God, that was itself God. *Memartyrēka hoti houtos estin ho huios tou theou* (v. 34), this is the issue in the knowledge that lies behind the *houtos ēn.* And in speaking as well as perceiving — *martyrei peri autou kai kekragen legōn* is the new thing compared to v. 14 — he *constitutes, he* constitutes — it is that simple! — the office of the New Testament witness, the apostolic office. Readiness is no longer all;[156] on the basis of the *etheasametha* the readiness becomes a leap, an action. The apostolic action, which, like the prophetic action, is only a pointer but a concrete pointer, is made possible and necessary by the incarnation of the Word: *houtos ēn.*

Note that this is how *John* saw John. This is how "the one, true, tender, and chief Gospel"[157] understood the Baptist. We should not fail to point out that it is surprising that it understood him thus. The Synoptics tell us about his witness as a forerunner and prophet but not about his recognition and confession of this *houtos ēn.* apart perhaps from the very cautious passage in Matt. 3:14 in which the Baptist says to Jesus: "I need to be baptized by you, and do you come to me?" over against which stands the question from prison in Matt. 11:3: "Are you he who is to come, or shall we look for another?" and especially Jesus' own saying in Matt. 11:11 about the least in the kingdom of heaven who is greater than John the Baptist. We may also think of the saying in Matt. 13:17 about the many prophets and righteous men who have not seen and heard

---

[156]Cf. Shakespeare's *Hamlet.* act v. scene 2: "The readiness is all."
[157]See Luther's preface to *Das Neue Testament Deutsch.* WA. DB. 6. p. 10.

what the disciples see and hear even though they longed to do so.
Perhaps in counterpoint to these passages there stands, when it is
rightly understood, that about storming the kingdom of heaven in
Matt. 11:12, and also that about the law and prophets who proph-
esied until John in Matt. 11:13f. But it is understandable if someone argues that on the basis of the Synoptics we should never think
of placing the Baptist alongside or among the apostles. All this,
however, does not alter the fact that the Fourth Evangelist does
think of doing this, and perhaps on the basis of the Synoptics! His
Baptist is a witness to both promise *and* fulfilment. He not only
prophesies Christ but also recognizes and confesses him. With a
strong foot (Grünewald) he stands resolutely on the soil of the New
Testament. It is not our task here to inquire how the church, which
recognized[158] both the Synoptics and John as canonical, obviously
reconciles these two portraits of the Baptist without expunging
their distinctive features. That would be a good and serious task
in New Testament theology, but it is not obligatory for us.[159] The
side-glance at the Synoptic portrait has simply served to remind us
that the Johannine portrait does in fact pose a problem for us.[160]

Formally we have still to say that the verse is naturally an
anticipation of v. 30. The prologue picks this fruitful element out
of the story of the Baptist. What is told in that story is here considered in advance and its significance in principle is estimated.
This explains why there we have *houtos estin* but here the strangely
retrospective *houtos ēn*, which undoubtedly, like the *ēn* of v. 9 and
v. 10, denotes, not his concrete existence and nature, but his historical appearance considered as a whole. Hence we should not
press the imperfect. This would lead to impossible constructions,
e.g., to the theory that a transfigured Baptist is here pointing from
the other world to an earthly appearance of the incarnate Logos
which is now past. Nor should we follow Zahn (again the incorri-
gible historicist) and juggle away the imperfect with the sophism

---

[158]A: "established."

[159]A adds: "And I want nothing whatever to do with research into the life
of Jesus, i.e., with the task of *critically* opposing the two portraits (or, what is
worse, comparing and *harmonizing* them)."

[160]A adds: "I must ask you, if what has been said does not please you, not
to hold it against me but against the Evangelist, whom we have to expound. *He*
says it, and he says it *thus.* Yet I cannot and will not deny that I think what he
says is *right.*"

that "was" and "is" amount to the same thing in this connection.[161]
There is undoubtedly a backward look. The pass from the Old
Testament to the New has been crossed. We stand on this side of
the epiphany. It is no longer the prophet but the apostle who is
now speaking, the prophet who has become an apostle, or the apostle who speaks out of the prophet, for whom the being of him who
comes is a completed fact. This does not exclude but includes the
fact that the *ēn*, corresponding to the *martyrei*, has the full present
force of the *estin* of v. 30.

16. **Hoti ek tou plērōmatos autou hēmeis pantes elabomen, kai
charin anti charitos.** "There can be no question but that the statement of the Baptist is restricted to v. 15," Zahn triumphantly declares.[162] He speaks in the name of almost all modern exegesis
from Cocceius by way of Bengel and Tholuck to present-day commentators. But the whole of the early church also had no doubt
that the Baptist's statement included vv. 15-18, so that the Baptist
utters the final words of the prologue, which the new beginning in
v. 19 fits in with so well that it is hard to see the break between
prologue and Gospel. The modern view seems to have against it
the connecting and explanatory *hoti* of v. 15. Or should we read
hoti kai with the Syriac and Antioch tradition, and most of the
Greek majuscules, against the Egyptian and Western texts, and ℵ
BCD? Zahn admits that this is not so well attested as one might
desire,[163] and W. Bauer rejects it as an obvious smoothing.[164] If in
spite of this we insist on taking the modern view, we are compelled
to view v. 15 as a parenthesis. Looking back beyond it, the Evangelist wants to explain the *plērēs charitos* of v. 14. It must be
conceded that there is a connection between vv. 16-18 on the one
side and v. 14 on the other. The taking up again of many terms
shows this: *plērōma, charis, alētheia, monogenēs, patēr, egeneto.*
But the connection may lie in the content and does not have to mean
that vv. 16-18 continue the Evangelist's presentation in v. 14. It
must also be allowed that the idea of explaining the *plērēs charitos*
of v. 14 makes good sense of v. 16. We have *perceived* the fulness
of grace in him as we have *received* of his fulness grace for grace.

---

[161]Zahn, op. cit., p. 88 n. 97.
[162]Zahn, op. cit., p. 90.
[163]Zahn, op. cit., p. 91 n. 3.
[164]Bauer, op. cit., p. 26.

This also yields an attractive parallel to vv. 12-13. But then vv. 17-18
are left hanging in the air. Whence and why is the antithesis developed in these final verses? With what inner necessity or credi-
bility are precisely these thoughts now introduced at the end of the
prologue? We search modern commentaries in vain for an illuminating answer to this question. But the situation is different, as we
shall see, if, ignoring that bedazzling parallel, we take vv. 17-18 as
well as v. 16 very naturally as part of the Baptist's speech. The
hēmeis of v. 14, which reappears, could be an argument against
this view only if with the *houtos ēn* of v. 15 the Baptist were not
stating something which he could say only as one of the *hēmeis* of
v. 14, as one of those who perceive. It is hard to see why, having
been allowed to speak in v. 15, and with no grammatical objection
apart from the change from the singular to the plural, he should
not be continuing to speak in their name. I think the aversion to
this view rests (1) on the prejudgment that the Baptist could not
and should not speak in such New Testament fashion as is found
here. Nevertheless, one must say, the speeches of the Baptist in
1:29ff. and 3:27ff. prove incontrovertibly that legitimately or not
he *does* this in John's Gospel. It rests (2) on a failure to understand
the representative position of the Baptist, especially in the prologue,
where it is appropriate that not merely in his own person, but as
the conductor of the Christian community in general and the apostolic and prophetic witnesses in particular, he should show how
they have come to be what they are. If we see this, if we pick up
again the dropped thread of ancient exegesis of this passage, then
(with the prologue) this ceases to be a general speech and proves
to be an inwardly organized and understandable pronouncement
which with full right stands in its own place. Naturally — and this
much must be granted at once to champions of the newer view —
we have to take it with a pinch of salt when vv. 16-18 are called
a continuation of the Baptist's address. Strictly even v. 15 is not a
reported address but a typical saying gathered from one or more
such addresses and quoted so as to recall in principle how, in
sum, the Baptist spoke. Naturally vv. 16-18 must be taken in the
same way whether we seek the source of the verses, as regards
both form and content, in some special tradition or reminiscence
or in the Evangelist himself. At all events, history is not *narrated*
here; it is *contemplated,* summarized, surveyed, and interpreted:
this was the relation of the Baptist to Christ. On the basis of his

recognition of the Incarnate, he, the prophet, the *anthrōpos apestalmenos para theou*, recognized him as the light that comes into the world, as the Word that was in the beginning. Renouncing any precedence over him or equality with him, confessing himself to be totally a recipient of revelation from him, he stands over against him, not as himself a revealer, not as the founder of a religion, not as the head of his own church, but in exactly the same way as do the disciples, the apostles, the author of the Gospel, and the Christian community at large. This is the content of vv. 16-18 in exposition of the basic statement in v. 15. Let us now consider v. 16 in detail.

Hoti ek tou plērōmatos autou hēmeis pantes elabomen, it says first. How are we to think of the link with v. 15 in the *hoti*, for which we have just decided? Calvin expresses it as follows: *"Nunc de Christi officio concionari incipit, quod bonorum omnium affluentiam in se contineat, ita ut non aliunde ulla pars salutis petenda sit."*[165] I think this interpretation is right; although Calvin later draws back at the decisive point, we might sum up the whole content of the verse in his terms: the *"non aliunde,"* the uniqueness of Christ as the place where salvation is to be found, is the point of the first clause in v. 16, the first reason why the Baptist pronounces his *houtos ēn* in v. 15 and calls this one the *prōtos*, which is the equivalent of the *monogenēs*, the bearer of *doxa*, the eternal Logos. (The second clause of v. 16 will give the second reason, the *"affluentia bonorum"* that is found in Christ.) Of *his* fulness we all have *received*. We have to say the same about the *elabomen* as about the *ēn* of v. 15. Naturally it is striking that the Evangelist has the Baptist speak in the past tense about his receiving, about his dependence on the incarnate Logos (as about the recognition of his presence in v. 15). Yet once again we should neither press this (e.g., historically, as though the Baptist at the moment of the confession were looking back to some earlier experiences with Jesus, which is ruled out completely by the double *kago ouk ēdein auton* of vv. 31 and 33) nor ignore it, which, now that we have the aorist, is even more impossible than in v. 15. All those who, with the Baptist (v. 15) or the Evangelist (v. 2), know and say *houtos ēn* are

---

[165]Calvin, op. cit., col. 16. [See Eng. tr. p. 23: "He now begins to preach about Christ's office, which contains such an abundance of all blessings that no part of salvation is to be sought elsewhere."]

people who thereby prove and confirm that they have received of
his fulness, that they have been put in a position to do so by a gift
(think of vv. 12-13). The emphasis is not on this, however, but on
what is expressed by the *autou* and the *hēmeis pantes*. The *pantes*
is not a strengthening of the *hēmeis* that we may clearly regard as
superfluous, but, and Zahn is certainly right here,[166] it has the
significance of an exclusive antithesis to the One; we others, all the
rest, all of us who precede or follow him, stand to him in an irre-
versible relationship, i.e., that of receiving what we have received
from *his* fulness. In ourselves we are *"spiritualium bonorum inopes
et vacui."* But we draw on the *"vere inexhaustus fons plenitudinis
Christi,"*[167] *ek plērōmatos autou*. As we receive in this way, from
a source which is not only a special one but the only available
source in which we can find *plērōma*, we are what we are. And
because we received thus, we say: *houtos ēn*. This is why he is for
us the *prōtos* (v. 15) before whom we bow and whom we serve. As
the term *plērōma* = *plērēs* already shows, we are right to connect
v. 16 with v. 14, not in such a way as to provide here a basis for
the *plērēs*, but in such a way that the perceiving of the glory of him
who is full of grace and truth, and hence the witnessing office that
is grounded in this perceiving, is now explained by the fact that
this fulness is in him *alone*, that those who perceive could not find
it elsewhere, that they did not bring anything of their own or from
any other source, that they were, then, truly recipients in the twofold sense that they themselves had nothing and that they could
not find anywhere else what they received here. We recall again,
even though it was spoken in another connection, the Pauline saying: *en autō katoikei pan to plērōma tēs theotētos* (Col. 2:9). This
exclusive explanation of their relationship to the divine *plērōma*
establishes, not the *plērōma* itself, but the need for the recognition
presupposed in v. 15: Because he is for the *hēmeis* not just *one*
source but the *only* source of *plērōma*, we say: *houtos ēn*. This is
why he is for them the *prōtos*. This is why the Baptist is subordinate. This is the reason for the unconditional respect with which
the Evangelist approaches his work. The exclusiveness of what
meets them in this person demands and establishes the exclusive-

---

[166]Zahn, op. cit., p. 92.
[167]Calvin, op. cit., col. 17. [See Eng. tr. p. 23: "the fulness of Christ, which
is . . . an inexhaustible fountain indeed."]

ness of this person and therefore of their attitude to this person. Certainly in the mind of the Evangelist one might reverse this statement. But in this place this is what he can say and wants to say.

Thus far the first clause. After *elabomen* we should put a comma. To be sure, *charin anti chariton* is the object of *elabomen*. Hence *elabomen* has to be firmly adduced to explain the second clause. But by the *kai* the object is so separated from the statement to which it undoubtedly belongs grammatically that we first have to take *elabomen* separately, generally, and with an indefinite object. The stress does not fall first either on the receiving itself or on its object. It falls solely and simply on the whence of receiving, and indeed on the exclusiveness of the whence. Of *his* fulness we have received. In relation to him we are all put in our proper place as recipients. But now, in a new beginning, in a second clause, we are told emphatically (this is the point of the *kai*) what we have received here: grace for grace. Concerning this formula there is a whole series of opinions. The best known is that of Augustine,[168] who is followed among modern expositors by, e.g., Cocceius, Schleiermacher, and Schlatter.[169] According to them *anti* has the force of "through" or "by means of," and the first time *charis* is the grace of eternal life granted by God, while the second time it is the grace of the believing also granted by God. The meaning is thus that we have received eternal life through believing. We have both the thing itself and the means thereto from God alone; we have grace through grace. *"Dona sua in nobis Deus coronat. Pie quidem id et scite dictum, sed ad praesentum locum minus apte,"* Calvin comments respectfully but correctly.[170] In itself, dogmatically, Augustine's fine interpretation is excellent, and it is not impossible in the context, but it gives too much force to the *anti,* so that, even if with regret, we have to abandon it. No matter how clearly Calvin sees the problem with the Augustinian explanation, however, he seems here, as in v. 4, not to have seen the beam in his own eye. For what he proposes in place of the rejected view is unfortunately

---

[168]Augustine, op. cit., III, 9 (pp. 39f.). [See Eng. tr. pp. 21f.]

[169]Cocceius, op. cit., p. 18; Schleiermacher, op. cit., pp. 37ff.; Schlatter, op. cit., pp. 8f.

[170]Calvin, op. cit., col. 17. [See Eng. tr. p. 24: "God . . . crowns His own gifts in us. This is a godly and wise observation, but it does not fit in with the present verse."]

no better: We received grace, grace ordained for us, *anti charitos*, i.e., through, or mediated by (*"tanquam per canalem"*) the grace loaned to Christ by his Father. *"Haec est unctio, qua delibatus fuit, ut nos secum omnes ungeret. Unde et ille Christus vocatur, nos Christiani."*[171] Again very fine and materially true, and again possible in the context, but again the *anti*, which has to denote an exchange or alternation, comes off much too badly to let us adopt this view. The *anti* is better evaluated in Chrysostom, Cyril, Theophylactus, Erasmus, Beza,[172] and others, who by the grace that replaces the other grace understand the New Testament replacing the Old. No objection can be brought against this interpretation on the basis of v. 17. For it is certain that the confrontation which that verse assumes between the law brought by Moses and the grace and truth that have come through Jesus Christ do not deny to the Old Testament, to the law, participation in grace and truth, so that in v. 16 we might very well speak in a special way, which has yet to be described, of the grace of the Old Testament. I need hardly show how well this understanding fits the context or what, if it were true, it would tell us about the exchanging of the prophetic for the apostolic offices and their common origin in the *plērōma autou*. Unfortunately this third interpretation is also not the right one. In Paul, it is true, *charis* can at times (e.g., in Gal. 2:9; Rom. 5:2; Phil. 1:7) denote the grace of apostolic office, but John is not Paul, and we have no parallel for the Old Testament grace even if we take that Pauline usage into account. Even as we reject them, we cannot deny that these older understandings have material power and truth and possible compatibility with the context. In contrast, the opinion of Zahn is a strange one when he takes *charis anti charitos* to signify the change in the gifts which the disciples received when they entered into fellowship with the incarnate Logos, namely, the change to revelation by the words and works of Christ.[173] Materially this is a not unimportant point when we consider the accounts assembled in the Synoptics and Acts, but I can only say that it is a thought that is alien to the text. A fifth possi-

---

[171]Calvin, op. cit., col. 18. [See Eng. tr. p. 24: "This is the anointing which was liberally poured upon Him that He might anoint us all along with Him. It is for this reason, too, that He is called Christ, and we, Christians."]

[172]All adduced by H. A. W. Meyer, op. cit., p. 78. [See Eng. tr. p. 68.]

[173]Zahn, op. cit., p. 93.

bility, which with Luther, Bengel, Meyer, Holtzmann, and W. Bauer[174] I regard as the necessary one, arises (1) when we do not start by thinking *charis* must have some special sense here but stay with what it usually denotes in John, and (2) when we do not start by thinking the second *charis* must be different from the first, but assume that materially we have the same grace in both instances. The *anti* can still signify an exchange or alternation, yet not that of different gifts received from the same fulness, but that of the same gift given and received different times — continuously, as we might at once perhaps interpret — and not becoming another gift but retaining its material identity — this is where the stress falls. This would be the nuance that I would find in the *"affluentia bonorum"* (Calvin), which is indeed at issue here. Other nuances are possible with this fifth understanding. To be complete, I will share two others. (a) With Meyer, Holtzmann, and Bauer, following a similar saying in Philo, one might lay emphasis on the fact that grace upon grace flows unceasingly upon the recipients like successive waves of the ocean, perhaps with the secondary sense that Bengel proposes: *"Proximam quamque gratiam satis quidem magnam gratia subsequens cumulo et plenitudine sua quasi obruit."*[175] (b) With Luther one might stress not so much the endless streaming *from the source* as the endlessness of the streaming *itself.* On this assumption Luther has a fine sermon on the text: "As the dear sun is not darkened by the fact that the whole world enjoys its light but could illuminate ten worlds, as a hundred thousand lights can be lit from one light and this would not affect the first light, as a learned man can make a thousand people learned, and the more he gives to others, the more he has himself — so Christ our Lord is an endless spring and fountain of all grace, truth, righteousness, wisdom, and life, having neither measure, end, nor source, so that even though the whole world draw enough grace and truth from him for all to become angels, yet he would still not lose a single drop: the

---

[174]Luther. WA 46. p. 654 (Eberle, p. 97) [see Eng. tr. pp. 135f. (cited in n. 39 above)] [Luther, however, speaks of a twofold grace. Christ's and ours]; Bengel, op. cit., p. 364 [see Eng. tr. vol. II. pp. 253f.]; Meyer, op. cit., p. 78 [see Eng. tr. p. 68]; Holtzmann. op. cit., p. 48; Bauer, op. cit., p. 27.

[175]Bengel, loc. cit. [See Eng. tr. vol. II, p. 253: "Each last portion of grace [though itself], indeed large enough, the subsequent grace by accumulation and by its own fulness, as it were, overwhelms [buries under the load of its own fulness]."]

source would still be overflowing with grace."[176] No serious conflict between (a) and (b) is necessary. Along with my own suggestion one might regard either of them with a good conscience as free from objection. Nevertheless, it should be said that perhaps we can stay closer to the text with the view that we receive grace and then grace again. The most exact sense seems to be that alternation of receiving caused no alternation of gift. A hundred experiments proved the same law, a hundred arguments established the same self-grounded thesis, a hundred ways all led to Rome. As recipients we stood constantly before the *affluentia* of the unity, which speaks on its own behalf and testifies that it is the truth.

What does the addition *kai charin anti charitos* mean in the context of the verse on the assumption that the third nuance of the fifth interpretation is correct? It is obviously a second definition of the way in which we have received. We have not just received from the fulness of the *One*, but, no matter who we are or how often we have received, we have received *one thing*. What touched us, what we took, what was given to us in all its greatness and strangeness, was grace, life wonderfully breaking into the world of death, re-demption. There were no vacillations, no more or less, no this way and that. With the exclusiveness of the whence is the exclusiveness of the what, of what is received. The two statements together es-tablish what the verse is seeking to establish in relation to v. 15. Here, as distinct from vv. 11 and 12, the *lambanein* totally reflects the receiving and not the taking. The reference is to what only God can give, and to the *constancy* with which this gift is one in spite of every alternation: *charis anti charitos*. It is to this as well as to the *uniqueness* of the place where we received it (to which the first part of the statement refers). Precisely with this constancy and uniqueness we recognized that it was given by God, and we rec-ognized him through whom we received it as the *prōtos*, as the bearer of *doxa*, as the eternal Logos. This explains the *houtos ēn*. This explains the subordination of the Baptist. This explains the attitude that the Evangelist adopts.

17-18. Hoti ho nomos dia Mōuseōs edothē, hē charis kai hē alētheia dia Iēsou Christou egeneto. Theon oudeis heōraken pōpote;

---

[176]M. Luther, *Auslegung des ersten und zweiten Kapitels Johannis in Pre-digten 1537 und 1538*, WA 46, p. 653 (quoted from Eberle, op. cit., pp. 96f.). [See Eng. tr. p. 134 (cited in n. 39 above).]

monogenēs theos ho ōn eis ton kolpon tou patros, ekeinos exēgēsato.
These two verses form a single unit like vv. 12-13. They are not
connected syntactically but they are linked by the parallelism, by
their common antithetical structure, and especially by their corresponding antithetical content. They form the end of the prologue.
We expect a concluding, decisive saying which will crown the train
of thought from vv. 14-16, and in some way match the loftiness of
the opening. We do not expect it in vain. What we now hear is
perhaps the most majestic thing in the whole prologue. But we
must wage a by no means easy battle against almost the entire
exegetical tradition before we can hear this. Let us plunge into the
thick of the problems.

How are we to take the underlying *hoti* here? Meyer and
Holtzmann find in it a contrasting underlining of the *charis anti
charitos* (v. 16).[177] But how far does this need to be underlined?
And how far do the ideas of vv. 17-18 serve to underline it? Much
nearer the mark are those who with Calvin, Schlatter, and Zahn
think that v. 17 is anticipating and answering a possible objection
that arises to v. 16.[178] What is certain — one has only to read the
verses to catch their natural flow — is that the stress in each is on
the second and positive statement, while the first, although it says
something very definite in its own place, is truly there only for the
sake of the second. If this observation is correct, then the point of
the two verses is that twice that which the second statements say
is set in a bright light and that to which the first statements refer
is automatically put in the shade, not intentionally, but through the
force of the juxtaposition which in this sense speaks for itself.
Hence the underlying *hoti* has reference, not to the first statements
nor to the antithesis as such, but to the second statements. We
should thus translate: "For whereas the law was given by Moses,
grace and truth have come through Jesus Christ," and then, corresponding in sense: "Whereas no one has seen God at any time,
the only-begotten, God, who is in the bosom of the Father, has
brought word about him." To what, then, does the *hoti* point? It
necessarily points to a thesis whose basis is established by the

---

[177]Meyer, op. cit., p. 78 [See Eng. tr. p. 68]; Holtzmann, op. cit., p. 48.
    [178]Calvin, op. cit., col. 18 [See Eng. tr. p. 24]; Schlatter, op. cit., p. 9; Zahn,
op. cit., p. 94.

statements when stressed in this way. This is not true in v. 16. The content of the second statements in vv. 17-18, however, is too parallel to that of v. 16 to be a basis for it. Vv. 17-18 might stand *alongside* v. 16, and their *hoti alongside* that of v. 16, and then in a new and double statement establish together with v. 16 and its *hoti* the same thing, namely, the point of v. 15, the *houtos ēn,* or the decisive *prōtos mou ēn.* There, on the occasion of the self-subordination of the Baptist, the question arises, which might be put to the Evangelist too, with what right there comes about this subordination of the one to the other, and if this is the case with the Baptist, the acknowledged prophet, how it stands in principle with all those whom one knows as servants and friends of God. There *are* authorized and enlightened people. The whole secret theme of the prologue is unrolled herewith. Are they all to be put in the shade with John the Baptist, or John the Baptist with them? The answer is an unambiguous Yes. Yes. *charis kai alētheia dia Iēsou Christou. ekeinos exēgēsato.* This is the situation. As v. 16 pronounced the same Yes from the standpoint of what the *hēmeis* of v. 14 received from Christ, the one thing from the One, vv. 17-18 now give the same answer in the form of an objective description of the position and function of the One. An answer or basis is given to v. 15 by the simple means of quietly putting what Christ is and does side by side with what Moses is and does. This juxtaposition is meant to speak for itself. And it does speak for itself when we see what is to be seen here. It is especially important, of course, that we should *not* see what is *not* to be seen, which, if we insist strongly on seeing it, can only conceal what is actually to be seen. We must be grateful particularly to Zahn that he has stressed so much that in these verses, as we mentioned already at v. 14, we have a reminiscence of Exod. 34.[179] To the question by what right those who are authorized and enlightened by God are subordinated even though they seem to stand by right *side by side* with Jesus Christ, vv. 17-18 reply by recalling what Moses did and how in doing it he was God's servant and friend. The situation of Moses is as the first statements say. The law was given by him (v. 17a = Exod. 34:1ff.), and the saying that directly precedes applies: No one will live who sees me (v. 18a = Exod. 33:20). Over against

---

[179]Zahn, op. cit., p. 81.

Moses stands the one through whom *charis kai alētheia* come. But according to Exod. 34:6 this is Yahweh himself. Can there be anything there but the subordination of those who are authorized and enlightened without at least some slight infringement upon Yahweh? Who can want to compete with Yahweh? That this reminiscence is present seems to me to be convincingly proved by the coincidence of the two texts at the three points of comparison: the function of Moses as the lawgiver, the impossibility of seeing God, and the two terms *charis* and *alētheia*. Even if there is room for doubt in relation to one of the points, the coincidence can hardly be accidental. Let us now turn to the details.

What is meant by *ho nomos dia Mōüseōs edothē*? It seems especially important to me to affirm that not a syllable here implies any disqualification of Moses or the law, and that not a syllable of what follows ("Grace . . .") is set in the relation of an adversary to them. There is no reason at all to find in the innocent *edothē* anything disparaging as compared to the *egeneto* of the second clause, and to infer from this, by the supposed criticism of the mission of Moses in the fact that the law is only "given," a significant contrast. What is there derogatory about the fact that the law was "given"? As though there were not many, many passages in the New Testament which say that grace is given! There is also no reason, second, to suppose that in the light of Christ Moses is criticized materially, or in content, or as regards the value or importance of his position. Why should he be? If we compare the other passages in the Gospel that speak about Moses, we see that for all the author's sharp polemic against the "Jews," which is on another level, that is far from his intention. In John Moses with his law is viewed favorably in his own place. As *Moses*, of course, and in *his own* place! In terms of this place he can occupy a position that is positively related to Christ, a position which renders all polemic against him superfluous. He himself accuses the Jews to the Father (5:45ff.). "If you believed Moses, you would believe me, for he wrote of me. But if you do not believe his writings, how will you believe my words?" We may add that in this Gospel there is no question of any criticism of other Old Testament men of God either. These men, too, occupy a positive position relative to Christ which obviates all polemic. The situation with them is as it was with Abraham, who "rejoiced that he was to see my day; and he saw it and was glad" (8:56). No less indisputably the Evangelist writes about

Isaiah in the less well-known 12:41: "He saw his [Christ's] glory
and spoke of him." Third, it is a mistake to look for this or that
that might distinguish the *nomos* unfavorably from grace and truth.
From the days of Augustine[180] until now all sorts of things have
been read in about the mere demands of the law, about its pointing
finger which simply shows the way but does not lead to the goal,
about its character as letter, about its purely figurative worship,
about its mere *"adumbratio bonorum spiritualium,"* as Calvin puts
it.[181] All this is good, but *ad praesentem locum minus apte.* For
what is there about such things here? It might play a big role in
Paul or Hebrews, but where does it figure in the train of thought
of this Gospel in such a way as to justify our introducing it without
further ado here? Why should not the little clause be simply saying
what it says with no hidden critical or polemical agenda, namely,
that Moses, the man of God, had his own place and function, that
through *him* the *law* was given? Just as John the Baptist gives his
witness and the Evangelist writes his *Gospel. Suum cuique!* We
must visualize the situation in Exod. 34, which the Evangelist undoubtedly has before him, in order to grasp that with this enough
is in fact said. There at God's command Moses cuts two tablets of
stone, rises up early in the morning, and goes to the top of the
mountain. This is Moses. But then Yahweh comes down to him in
the cloud, passes before him, and speaks the words about his grace
and faithfulness. This is Yahweh. "And Moses made haste to bow
his head toward the earth, and worshiped" (v. 8). This is Moses
again. It is thus that he gets the law, thus that it is given to him.
"The law was given by Moses" means that Moses did what Moses
could do in his place and on his level as a mediator of revelation.
But in his place, in his sphere, he is on the human side over against
God, a mediator of revelation only insofar as he is first a recipient.
Without any criticism of Moses or his law, an order is thus established in the sense of v. 15: *"Non sibi aliquid amplius servus as-
signet, quam quod per illum factum est. Electus ad magnum
ministerium tamquam fidelis in domo, sed tamen servus, agere*

---

[180]Augustine, op. cit., III, 11-13 (pp. 41-43). [See Eng. tr. pp. 22f.]

[181]Calvin, op. cit., col. 18. [See Eng. tr. p. 24: "outlined image of spiritual
blessings."]

secundum Legem potest, solvere a reatu Legis non potest. "[182] The law is not what will later be said to come through Jesus Christ. It is not grace and truth. Naturally not; nor is it the witness of the Baptist nor John's Gospel!

But what reason is there to set these things, which lie on a different level, in an adversative relation to grace and truth? As though mentioning them in the same breath were not enough to make their relationship clear. Where is the *men . . . de* or the *alla* which would be needed if John meant things differently? Certainly there is contrast, but with no trace of polemic it simply says: *hē charis kai hē alētheia dia Iēsou Christou egeneto.* This is the main point. This by itself is the basis of the *houtos ēn* and the *prōtos mou ēn* of v. 15. Grace and truth — note the solemnity which the use of the article gives these terms here — life and light, redemption and revelation, no, these do not come through Moses any more today than they did on Sinai, excellent though he with his stone tablets may be in his place, serving before God and serving God as is proper for a man, receiving and passing on God's Word, *peri Christou graphōn* [cf. John 5:46]. Grace and truth, according to Exod. 34, come absolutely and exclusively through the mouth of Yahweh himself. "I am of great grace and faithfulness," is what Yahweh the Giver of revelation has to say about himself to Moses its recipient (and as such the mediator of the law). Exactly in the place where Yahweh stood, there stands here the one to whom the *houtos ēn* of v. 15 applies. Exactly in the function in which Yahweh acted there, he acts here. Through him grace and truth come, or come about, or come on the scene — the *egeneto* has this historical sense here as in v. 6, although naturally we have to think also of the great principial *egeneto* of v. 14 — through him! Hence grace and truth do indeed stand in contrast with the law and he with Moses. But how? Again: "Moses made haste to bow his head toward the earth and worshiped" [Exod. 34:8]. It is a complete misunderstanding of the situation and its characteristic distances to think in terms of religious comparison or even of the distinction between the economy of the Old Testament and that of the New.

---

[182]Augustine, op. cit., III, 16 (cf. p. 44). [See Eng. tr. p. 23: "Let not the servant attribute to himself more than was done through him. Chosen to a great ministry as one faithful in his house, but yet a servant, he is able to act according to the law, but cannot release from the guilt of the law."]

This should be clear. The Old and New Testaments, the prophets and apostles, are not here compared, nor is it considered what might be the difference between the seeing of *doxa autou* by Isaiah and by the *hēmeis* of v. 14 insofar as the Evangelist is thinking of himself and his Christian contemporaries. Compared here are the bearer of the *doxa* himself and other men of God. It seems as though the bearer of the *doxa* is in the same series as they are. The problem is how there can be among those in the same series the kind of subordinate relationship that is envisaged in v. 15. The result of the comparison is established as soon as it is made. When heaven is compared to earth, or grace and truth are compared to the law, or Jesus Christ is compared to Moses, then ipso facto their incomparability or incommensurability is immediately apparent. The result is not that Christ is victorious in the competition but that there is no competition. This was the meaning of the *prōtos mou ēn* of v. 15, as we saw. This is what is now said by way of providing a basis for v. 15.

Note also that here for the first time, and quite incidentally as it would seem, the name of Jesus Christ occurs. Here for the first time! It cannot be contested that for sixteen whole verses the Evangelist not only could be speaking about Jesus Christ but that he obviously intended to do so, although without presenting and commending him as a "historical personality" in the glowing terms which in modern times claim to be the only ones that do justice to the New Testament.[183] Why this name precisely at this point? Obviously mention of the human name of Moses evokes the mention of this other name. And precisely when one notes the reminiscence of Exod. 34 it is, of course, highly significant that as the name of this other through whom grace and truth come, the name of the Logos is not repeated — it finally drops out of the picture with v. 14 — but this human name: Jesus the Messiah. The whole paradox of the *ho logos sarx egeneto,* which dominates this second part of the prologue, comes with double force to the forefront with the mention of this name in *this* context and along with *this* Old Testament reminiscence, and not, in truth, incidentally, but in deliberate fashion and after long restraint. For Jesus the Messiah stands where Yahweh stood. And as Moses, the bringer of the law, stood

---

[183]A: "In the glowing pietistic terms with which we are plagued on all sides today."

over against Yahweh, no, lay on the earth before him as a recipient
of revelation, so, and not otherwise, the Baptist and the Evangelist
stand over against Jesus Christ. So much, in this sense, do they in
fact stand relentlessly and definitively in the shade. This is how it
is in principle with all of us, even those who are authorized and
enlightened by God, even though they carry the tablets of the law
or the scroll of the Gospel under their arms, with the Baptist between them. Only worship and service are in place here. *Hence*
v. 15.

Let us now turn to the second antithesis in v. 18. What is
meant by *theon oudeis heōraken pōpote*? Precisely what is said, we
may again reply. The lack of an article before *theos* shows that as
in v. 1c and v. 18b we are dealing with the essence of God. God's
essence is not seen. God is sometimes seen in other ways, in manifestations of his essence. "Moses saw a cloud, he saw an angel, he
saw fire: these are mere creatures: they were a picture of the Lord,
but did not grant the presence of the Lord himself."[184] Not a vision
of the *doxa theou*, we are tempted to add, inasmuch as the *doxa*
is God's essence in its visibility. But John seems to have something
higher than *doxa* in view here. The glory of God is perceived (v. 14)
and even sometimes seen (11:40; 12:41; cf. also *theōrein tēn doxan*,
17:24). The Son alone sees the Father (6:46), and yet so do those
who see the Son (14:7, 9), and on the same condition there is a
theōrein ton pempsanta me (12:45). (The extreme limit seems to
be indicated by Matt. 5:8 with its *ton theon opsontai*, where one
should note the definite article and the undoubtedly eschatological
future.) What we do not have, whether as *horan* or *theōrein* or
theasthai, is the seeing of him who, or that which, is here called
theos. No one sees God; cf. 1 John 4:20, and explicitly the *theon
oudeis pōpote tetheatai* of 1 John 4:12. As *theos* he who as Father
may be seen in the Son, and whose glory reveals itself and is perceived, is *aoratos*, invisible (Rom. 1:20; 1 Tim. 1:17; Heb. 11:27;
*phōs oikōn aprositon, hon eiden oudeis anthrōpōn oude idein dy-
natai*, 1 Tim. 6:16). It strangely contradicts John's Gospel, and the
rest of the New Testament, if, with most exegetes, we take Rom.
1:20 to refer to seeing the invisible God and not to perceiving his
invisibility, the mystery of his hiddenness in the works of creation.

---

[184]Augustine, op. cit., III, 17 (p. 45). [See Eng. tr. p. 23.]

Oudeis, as in 1 John 4:20; 1 Tim. 6:16, naturally means no human being. The emphasis in the first statement is on this *oudeis* as a negative human determination. This may be seen from the second statement, where unquestionably the *ekeinos,* which is characterized as divine by the three definitions *monogenēs, theos,* and *ho ōn eis ton kolpon tou patros,* carries the stress. *Horan,* as distinct from intuitional *theasthai,* means simple, direct, objective seeing. In John this cannot be limited to physical seeing, although we have to start out with this basic sense. Beyond that we have also to think of objective recognition, which may be a purely mental act. Such *horan theon* in the narrower or broader sense is not given to any human, says the verse. Calvin and Cocceius were certainly not on the right track when they tried to relativize or reinterpret the statement as meaning that the fathers did not have the full knowledge of God that the Gospel now gives. *"Illi parvas tantum vivae lucis scintillas habebant, cuius plenus hodie fulgor nos illustrat."*[185] *"Non viderunt gloriam Dei maximam; non viderunt Deum iustificantem improbum."*[186] Luther better perceived that we have here an absolute contrast, that the question is whether we can know God by our natural powers, to which he gave the prophetic answer that this question will again cause much grief.[187] Naturally, the reference in the *oudeis heōraken* is not just to a lack that can be made good by revelation. This is shown by the express *oudeis pōpote* (no one at any time!) both here and in 1 John 4:12; it should be noted that the perfect *heōraken* (like the *kekragen* of v. 15) has here present or supratemporal significance, so that it is not part of a narrative but is presenting a universal fact. The whole statement, with its full content, applies also to those who hear and believe and proclaim the gospel. The second statement does not say that he has enabled us to see or perceive God. It is still true that no one ever sees God. An interesting question arising out of Matt. 5:8 is whether the statement still retains its validity with reference to eternal redemption. Medieval theology denied this and ascribed to the blessed in heaven, in distinction even from the angels, an immediate vision

---

[185]Calvin, op. cit., col. 19. [See Eng. tr. p. 26: "For they had nothing more than little sparks of that light of life whose full brightness lightens us today."]

[186]Cocceius. op. cit., p. 20 [Eng. tr.: "They did not see the full glory of God; they did not see the God who justifies the wicked."].

[187]Luther, WA 46, p. 667 (Eberle, p. 98). [See Eng. tr. pp. 149f. (cited in n. 39 above).]

of the divine essence.[188] But it, too, taught that on earth this direct vision is not granted even to the prophets. And this is the issue in the present passage.

In the negative statement of v. 18 we are no more to seek a disqualification than in v. 17a. The lack, which can be made good only eschatologically, and which means that we cannot see God or perceive him objectively, is a matter apart which is not the true issue here. We must turn once again to the passage in Exod. 33:18ff., which is normative for an understanding of this whole section. Moses prays God, "Show me thy glory." The Lord answers: "I will make all my goodness pass before you, and will proclaim before you my name. I will be gracious to whom I will be gracious, and will show mercy on whom I will show mercy. But you cannot see my face; for man shall not see me and live." Moses then receives the command to put himself in a cleft of the rock. When the glory of the Lord passes by, he, the Lord, will cover him with his hand until he has passed by. "Then I will take away my hand, and you shall see my back; but my face cannot be seen." The obvious meaning is that because we are human we can none of us see God's face. Not even those who are prophets! Not even the man called Moses! *Oudeis pōpote.* One has to say that we have here an essential theological determination of humanity. Something is brought to light which refers not only to God but also, on our own level, to us. We are as we are. To see God would, strictly, mean our destruction, our dissolution as such. "Man shall not see me and live." If in v. 17a the simple affirmation that Moses is the lawgiver might still be ambivalent, v. 18a shows quite unequivocally how it is even with those who are authorized and enlightened by God. They, too, stand under the human conditions which are also pitiless limits. This essential determination of humanity in relation to God, great though the distinctions may be in detail, distinctions of service within this relation, sets them all in principle on the same level. No matter what they become, or how wonderfully God may use them, or how much or how little, seeing God from behind in the cleft of

---

[188]Cf. Thomas Aquinas, *Summa Theologica.* III, suppl. qu. 92 a. 1; Benedict XII, Constitution *Benedictus Deus* (1336) in H. Denzinger and A. Schönmetzer, eds., *Enchiridion Symbolorum.* 33rd ed., 1965, No. 1000 (No. 530 in older editions of Denzinger). [See the English translation by R. J. Deferrari, *The Sources of Catholic Dogma* (St. Louis/London, 1957), No. 530.]

the rock, they are able or manage to grasp of him, one thing is certain, namely, that none of them, in general or in particular, finally sees or knows or understands anything of God, of the essence or substance or being of God, of his *theiotēs*. And this limit of their humanity is so strong that precisely in the relation to God which is in view in the *prōtos mou ēn* (v. 15) there can be no sub- or superordination, so little can his role as mediator of the law give to Moses any such precedence. But this does not apply to the relation between the witness John and Jesus Christ to whom he bears witness. What, then, does?

The second statement replies with no adversative particle and with mute and simple eloquence: *monogenēs, theos ho ōn eis ton kolpon tou patros, ekeinos exēgēsato.* The *monogenēs*, as we have seen in v. 14, is a stronger form of the term "son" and expresses the uniqueness with which an only son is related to his father, is close to him, knows him, and is his representative and heir. Everything that this conclusion to the prologue has to say converges on this uniqueness. The point is, in the light of v. 15, that Jesus, who as the incarnate seems to be one among equals with the Baptist and the Evangelist, or at best the first among equals, is to be described — since it is the Logos who became flesh — as an *ens sui generis* before whom, not arbitrarily nor in deification of a creature, but in worship of God, all others must yield. Although he is among others, shares their nature, and is flesh, he is not of the same order. The objection that the subordination of others to him which is envisaged in v. 15 is impossible because all flesh, in spite of relative distinctions, is in solidarity over against God — v. 18a shows in what respect — this objection does not apply to him. The solidarity is broken and removed by the fact that he, the *Logos*, became flesh. While standing among others, he really stands over against them. The full concreteness of the situation on Sinai between Moses and Yahweh has been brought to light by the fact that the Word became flesh. Where Moses reminds all of us of our *human* essence, so that we have to stand alongside all others, this one, who stands and goes as man among us, stands at the side of *God*. He is like an island in the ocean, one might say, which suddenly arises on the horizon where we see only wave after wave. This discovery and recognition of the unheard-of exception in the midst of the regularity, among all that is called flesh, is the motive force behind the *houtos ēn* of v. 2 and v. 15. Here revelation is not received and passed on as with Moses, and as is proper for human beings. Here, as the presupposition of all such receiving and passing on — and this is the problem of the Baptist and the Evangelist! — revelation is *given*, as is proper for God. The law can be given by human beings when *charis kai alētheia* come through God. This is their function. Only through God, however, do *charis kai alētheia* themselves come.

The phrases that follow, *theos* and *ho ōn eis ton kolpon tou patros*, define the main term *monogenēs* more closely. We are to read *theos* and not *huios*, although attestation for the latter is good and some of it old. But it seems to have arisen through a need to assimilate the formula to that of John 3:16, 18; 1 John 4:9, probably to avert Gnostic speculations about a *theos monogenēs*. There is no question of any such here. We do not read *ho monogenēs theos*, as though one of the gods, or, nonsensically, the one God were called *monogenēs*. Nestle's omission of the comma is misleading here. We have the same *theos* without the article as in v. 1c and v. 18a. The only-begotten is God by nature. He shares the divine essence which no one without exception either sees or knows. We are not told that he is the exception, that he sees and knows *theon*, but more simply and strongly that he is *theos*, that he is there where none of us can see. For this reason he differs from all the rest of us. For this reason, as is then said, he is able to *exēgeisthai*, tell us about God, be God's interpreter, as none of us can, i.e., originally as the pure Giver, to whom we are absolutely subject as bearers of the law or gospel, as recipients, as those who simply pass it on.

The second definition stresses that he is where none of us is: *ho ōn eis ton kolpon tou patros*. The *ōn* is usually taken to mean that now, at the time the Evangelist is writing, he is again in the place from which he came, in the bosom of the Father. On this view the Incarnation is an episodic interruption, as it were, of his true, original, and final being. I think that this overdramatic understanding robs the clause of its force. If according to the unanimous view of Zahn, Schlatter, Holtzmann, and Bauer[189] the reading *ho ōn en tō ouranō* is genuine in 3:13, the other idea is shown there to be Johannine, namely, that the Son does not cease to be *en tō ouranō* with his *katabainein*. Naturally not as *sarx* — this exagger-

---

[189]Zahn, op. cit., p. 201; Schlatter, op. cit., p. 30; Holtzmann, op. cit., p. 88; Bauer, op. cit., p. 53.

ation led later to the Lutheran doctrine of ubiquity — but as Logos. The possibility of this distinction must be left open here. Having become totally flesh on earth, he is totally with God in heaven. Unless we open the door to totally strange kenotic ideas, how could there be any break? As we saw in v. 14, his Incarnation means no limitation of his being as Logos. In vv. 1 and 2 his being as Logos includes being *pros ton theon.* This is what the present clause also says. *Ho theos* in distinction from *theos* without the article means the same as *ho patēr,* i.e., the divine person or subject who reveals himself in Christ or is revealed by him. Over against him as a second person, as the Son, or, more strongly, simply the *mono-genēs,* stands the person or subject who reveals him, or in or through whom he reveals himself, the bearer of *doxa,* the bringer of redemption and revelation, of grace and truth. Yet not over against him as we are over against him, as strangers, as those who cannot see or know him, who have first to receive revelation from him, but in such a way — as the *pros ton theon* of vv. 1 and 2 expresses — that he is at home with him, that he knows the Father as a child knows its father, that he lies on his bosom. In the accusative *eis* we are no more to seek the thought of turning to or dealings with or the like than we are in the *pros* of vv. 1 and 2. In Koine Greek *eis* often stands for *en,* and here it simply answers the question: Where? He who reveals stands over against him whom he reveals in such a way that to reveal him he has only to reveal himself. "Whoever sees me, sees the Father" [John 14:9]. This — his full and adequate representation of him whom he reveals, the Father — this is what lifts him absolutely out of the ranks to which all others belong. The Word became *flesh.* Yes, but it was the *Word* that became flesh. It is as such that he stands before us with his communication: *ekeinos exēgēsato. Exēgeisthai* is a technical term for the work of priests and soothsayers who communicate divine secrets.[190] The stress is not on the fact that he does *that* or that he *does* that. Others can do that, and do do it, without breaking the rule of v. 18a. The final word of the prologue is that *he* is the exegete, the communicator, the one with whom we have to do, he who is the *monogenēs,* whose information about himself is original, primary, and authentic revelation. *Ekeinos, he* is the *monogenēs.*

---

[190]Bauer, op. cit., p. 28.

God by nature, who is in the bosom of the Father. He, *this ekeinos*, definitively establishes the validity of the *houtos ēn* of vv. 1 and 2, the validity of the witness of John, both the Baptist and the Evangelist.

VERSES 19-34

And this is the witness of John when the Jews sent priests and Levites to him from Jerusalem to ask him: Who are you? Then he confessed and denied not, no, he confessed: I am not the Messiah. And they asked him: What then? Are you Elijah? And he said: I am not. Are you the prophet? And he answered: No. Then they said to him: Who are you? so that we may give an answer to those who sent us. What do you say about yourself? He said: I am the voice of one crying in the wilderness, Make straight the way of the Lord, as Isaiah the prophet said. And they were sent by the Pharisees. And they asked him and said to him: Why are you baptizing then if you are neither the Messiah, nor Elijah, nor the prophet? John answered them and said: I baptize with water. Among you stands one whom you do not know, he who comes after me, whose shoes' thongs I am not worthy to unloose. This took place at Bethany beyond the Jordan, where John was baptizing.

The next day he sees Jesus coming to him and says: There is the Lamb of God which takes away the sins of the world. This is he of whom I said: After me comes the man who ranks before me, because he was before me. And I did not know him, but I came baptizing with water so that he might be made known to Israel. And John bore witness and said: I saw the Spirit come down as a dove from heaven, and it rested upon him. And I did not know him. But he who sent me to baptize with water said to me: He on whom you see the Spirit come down and rest upon him, he it is who baptizes with the Holy Spirit. And I have seen and bear witness: This is the Son of God.

Vv. 19-34 clearly form a single complex in meaning. On the basis of v. 19 I would entitle it "The Witness of John." If our present interpretation of the prologue is right, then it cannot be contested that the prologue is organically and significantly related to this beginning of the Gospel proper. Our discussion of the problem of witness within a presentation in principle of the main theme of the Gospel has prepared us for the story that is told in these verses. Preceding the history of the incarnate Word there now follows the history of the witness. With deliberate concentration and one-sidedness it is the history of witness as such in the narrowest sense of the term. The Baptist's pre-history, his message of repentance and judgment, his sinister end — the Synoptists find a place for these and show some interest in them, but not this Evangelist. No, *hautē estin hē martyria tou Ioannou. martyria* understood in the strict sense of the prologue, *martyria peri tou phōtos* (v. 7), *martyria peri autou* (v. 15). What about this? What is there to tell? There are two clearly discernible parts. First vv. 19-28 tell us what the Baptist's witness was to himself, the shadow cast by the light. Then vv. 29-34 contain the witness proper, namely, the Baptist's witness to Jesus. Both sections divide fairly obviously into two subsections. In vv. 19-23 the Baptist explains what he is not and answers the question formulated in v. 22: *ti legeis peri seautou?* Over against this in vv. 24-28 is the answer to the question of v. 25: *ti oun baptizeis?* Then in vv. 29-31 we have the saying about the Lamb of God and the *houtos estin* and its explanation. Over against this in vv. 32-34 is the grounding of these sayings in the witness to the descent of the Spirit on Jesus. It is not ruled out that [between] v. 23 and v. 24 on the one side and v. 31 and v. 32 on the other there is a literary joint. The sudden mention of the Pharisees in v. 24 and the new start in v. 32 are at any rate surprising. On this thesis we have two parallel accounts that supplement each other. But it must be observed with W. Bauer that the reciprocal supplementing of these parts of the two sections is so good that we may quietly assume that we are dealing with what is now in fact a literary unity.[1] Note that the first parts of the two sections strictly contain two thoughts or at least one thought in two expressions or with two points: in vv. 19-23 the negations and the positive answer

---

[1] W. Bauer, op. cit., p. 12.

of the Baptist, in vv. 29-31 the saying about the Lamb of God and the *houtos estin* and explanation. If this is so, we have two series of three thoughts each, and in the following survey of the whole I will try to show that in each case I am dealing with the two series together, the witness of John to himself and his witness to Jesus. I would not venture to maintain that the correspondence and mutual elucidation of the two parts are deliberately intended by the author. I simply affirm that they are in fact present to some extent and that a synopsis of this kind is the simple way to gain a brief but comprehensive understanding of the text as a whole.

The first item, which unquestionably speaks for itself, is the threefold statement in vv. 19-21: I am not the Messiah, I am not Elijah, I am not the prophet. "The Jews" in John are usually a hostile group that we cannot pin down concretely, but in v. 19 they are fairly clearly the spiritual leaders and spiritual-secular authorities which represent the Jewish nation and have their seat in Jerusalem. These have sent a delegation of priests and Levites to the Baptist. According to Zahn, who is always very concrete, the Levites are to be regarded as police accompanying the priests in the dangerous Jordan region.[2] This delegation puts the question: Who are you? The meaning is: What is your religious mission and position (according to your own claim, as v. 22 shows)? To what category do you think you belong? The second and third questions are positive: Are you Elijah? Are you the prophet? The first time the Baptist does not wait for a positive question of this kind but answers (note how fully this answer is introduced in v. 20; this shows how important it is for the Evangelist): I am not the Messiah. What he thus denies is plainly what has been expected from him, the presupposition that surrounds him in the judgment of the people and perhaps in narrower or broader circles of readers of the Gospel. That the Baptist himself, as Zahn thinks,[3] was tempted to regard himself or to claim that he was the Messiah is a thought that is very alien to this Gospel. However that may be, the story of the Baptist begins with this vigorous negation. Its content is self-evident according to the prologue. The two ensuing negations give more food for thought. According to Matt. 11:14; 17:11f. Jesus himself calls the Baptist the coming Elijah. Although the prologue

---

[2] T. Zahn, op. cit., p. 112.
[3] Zahn, op. cit., p. 113.

offers no premises for the idea, he might also have been the "prophet" who according to Deut. 18:15 was expected along with the Messiah and as the precursor of the Messiah. In Matt. 11:9 Jesus himself even calls him *perissoteron prophētou.* Why is he neither Elijah nor the prophet? Does not the incident itself (cf. v. 23 and v. 31) give him the role either of the one or the other as he announces the coming of the Messiah? I find the best answer in Calvin: The Baptist claims no mandate or separate function of his own. He is *"subalternus tantum magister,"* and his teaching *"quaedam duntaxat audiendi alterius magistri praeparatio."*[4] Hence the second and third negations are a distinctive strengthening of the first. He is not only not the Christ; he is also not one of the traditional secondary figures. He is not a figure with saving significance. He does not have the role of such a figure in salvation history. The person who really has such a role, who is really perhaps Elijah or the prophet, does not know and does not want it. This person simply is it because it is given to him to be it. A real witness always is so against his own judgment. Note the distinctive strengthening of the second and third negations by the double *kagō ouk ēdein auton* in v. 31 and v. 33, about which we shall have to speak later. The continuation of the question in v. 22 shows us (I will not say with Zahn the indifference,[5] but) the embarrassment which arises around the witness, who does not fit into any category, who claims for himself neither, as suspected, the ultimate dignity nor even a penultimate dignity.

Let us set alongside this the first thing that the Baptist says about Jesus in v. 29: This is the Lamb of God which takes away the sin of the world. This is the light which casts the shadow that lies on the Baptist. This is the fulness which makes understandable and necessary the strange emptiness of his position. The bitter earnestness of the negation seems to be demanded in view of this. Of course, just coming from the prologue, we are a little puzzled. Jesus the Revealer dominates the picture and the inquiry there. Here it seems to be quite different. Here he is the one who takes away the sin of the world, and he does so as the Lamb, the Lamb

---

[4]J. Calvin, op. cit., cols. 21f. Calvin has *"subalternus tantum minister."* [See Eng. tr. p. 28: "an assistant minister . . . only a sort of preparation for listening to another teacher."]

[5]Zahn, op. cit., p. 116.

of God. But for John the two things are very closely related. Cf. 1 John 3:5: Jesus is manifested *hina tas hamartias arẹ̄*. This parallel also shows that *airein* here really means "to remove," "to carry off," "to take away." Why must that take place? The remarkable designation of Jesus as the Lamb of God gives an indirect answer to this question. We might think of Isa. 53:7. With more certainty we gather from John 19:36 that John, like Paul, sees in Jesus the fulfilment of the Passover lamb whose blood ensured the safety of the Israelites on the night when death smote the firstborn of Egypt. And this brings us back to the prologue, namely, to the probably related concepts of *charis* and *zōē* which are so significant there. If we are right, these are the content of *alētheia* and *phōs*, i.e., of revelation. In v. 16 *charis* with its content even came to the forefront for a moment. It is about this content of revelation that v. 29 speaks. Because of sin the world has fallen victim to death. But there is the Lamb, offered up by God himself, which takes sins — the participial clause *ho airōn* is probably no longer a figure but has the further material sense — which takes them away. It is possible that this *airein tēn hamartian* is a deliberate development of the *pherein* and *anapherein* of Isa. 53. This taking away took place in the blood, in the death of the Lamb. Redemption, *zōē*, life through righteousness, righteousness through judgment, judgment through vicarious sacrifice, vicarious sacrifice through God's own act — this is the train of thought. That the Baptist's first word about Jesus is also at once the last that is to be spoken about him, that the Christmas message at once becomes the message of the passion, this is beyond question. I must again refer to Grünewald and say: This Baptist, the one who knows, is the one who speaks here, the Baptist who also knows, who is the first to know, what the apostles know. Again, it is in this light, and perhaps only in this light, that one can understand the emphatic *ouk eimi*. What can *this* Baptist say except: "He must increase, but I must decrease" [John 3:30].

Let us return to the self-witness of vv. 22-23. If he does *not* want to be all those things that he is thought to be, he has to say *what* he wants to be. He thus replies from Isa. 40:3: I am the voice of one crying in the wilderness. This is the *positive* answer. Note the abbreviating of the Old Testament text. There is no mention of preparing the way, no reference to the coming glory of the Lord. Only the most necessary thing is said about what the voice cries.

John wants to be a voice crying in the wilderness. This is his whole function. He wants to be nothing but the bearer of his calling. He wants to be less as a person the more highly he thinks of his calling.[6] And yet the picture is now different from what it was. We now see the fulness, the positive implications, of that threefold denial. Those who have ears to hear, let them hear! Here is one who cries (*kekragen*, v. 15). If he is not any of the things that people think he is, as one who cries he is enigmatic in his anonymity; he cries in the desert. Yet he *does* cry. He *has* something to cry. He comes from a *Lord* whose way he must prepare and who might himself come on this way.

The enigma of the anonymity of this crying voice is not solved but is shown to be necessary when we look at vv. 30-31. Here an anonymity is *lifted*, namely, that of the Unique One among the many who come after John the Baptist, of him who is superior in principle to him and to all others because—as we have now to supply from v. 23—he is the Kyrios whose way the Baptist must prepare, who is thus the reason for the Baptist's own mission. *Houtos estin*: Jesus, who comes to him at a particular place (v. 28) on a particular day (v. 29). And now note—we have expressly discussed v. 30 in relation to v. 15—the continuation of v. 31: *kagō ouk ēdein auton.* This is emphatically repeated in v. 33. The Baptist does not think—this agrees with vv. 20-31—that he has some agreement with the Coming One, that he stands in a reciprocal relation to him, that he can as it were condition him as he is conditioned by him. No, the great, irremovable barrier of v. 18a is in force here. The conditioning relationship is not reversible. I did not know him—but (this *alla* is important here, as later in v. 33) because he is *there* and *must* be manifested to Israel, therefore I have my mission, therefore I have come with my water baptism. *I* am conditioned by *him* and not vice versa. *My* baptism is the complement of *his* baptism. I do not stand in the air but on solid ground because he who comes after me holds me with *his* action. The voice that cries in the wilderness has force and meaning, not on its own account (in itself it is, as it were, toneless) but in view of its object, through him who commands it to cry. And he is there. All the more, then, it, too, has to be there and wants to be there, but anony-

6Zahn, op. cit., p. 115.

mously. *"Sola enim est dei vocatio, quae legitimos ecclesiae minis-
tros facit."*[7]
    Vv. 24-28 deal with this legitimacy of the Baptist's vocation —
we turn again to the first narrative series. Let us ignore the debate
whether, with Schlatter and Zahn,[8] we are really, on the basis of
v. 24, to understand the question of v. 25 historically as a characteristic Pharisaic question. What is certain is that John's baptizing,
mentioned here for the first time, seems to his questioners, at least
in the mind of the Evangelist, to be the outcome and expression of
some dignity of the Baptist, of his character as a "public person."[9]
If he is not raising the claim to such a character (the question of
v. 25), if he does not seem to possess it, then by what right does
he baptize? What legitimacy at all does his activity have? It is
incorrect to say with the patristic expositor Heracleon[10] that in
vv. 26-27 the Baptist does not answer the question that is put but
says what he wants to say. What he says is as precisely as possible
an answer to the question of the legitimacy of his baptism. *I* baptize
with *water* — and now note that, as in vv. 17 and 18 there is no
adversative *de* or the like to form an antithesis — among you stands
the one whom you do not know. The stress is on the *mesos hymōn
stēkei.* He is *there,* the one for whose sake baptism with water
takes place and has to take place. Of course: *hon hymeis ouk oidate.*
You see my baptism with water, you know this side of the sacrament, its earthly matter, but you do not know its heavenly matter,
the baptizing of him who stands among you. For you do not know
him who gives meaning to my baptism, who is the reason for it.
Hence I can only say to you — and I say it as the answer to your
question — he is *there* among you. And now, corresponding to what
was developed in principle in vv. 15-18, there follows the strongest
possible delimitation of his own person and work compared to
those of the hidden one who is present. He is the one who comes
after me, who according to your judgment stands in my shadow —
yet I am not worthy to untie the thongs of his sandals. It does not

    [7]Calvin, op. cit., col. 27. [See Eng. tr. p. 34: "For it is only the calling of
God that makes regular ministers of the Church."]
    [8]A. Schlatter, op. cit., p. 12; T. Zahn, op. cit., p. 117.
    [9]Calvin, op. cit., col. 23. [See Eng. tr. p. 29.]
    [10]Cited in Bauer, op. cit., p. 32.

seem wise to me to say with W. Bauer[11] that v. 26 leads us to
suspect that the Baptist has nothing to do with messianic or Christian baptism. On the contrary, I would say that vv. 26 and 27 show
to what extent he does have to do with it, namely, to the extent that
even messianic baptism, the baptism of the Christian church, water
baptism, is not just the work of the Holy Spirit but is also the work
of the church's ministry and therefore of a human ministry. Here
again Calvin offers the apt explanation: *"Spiritualis Christi bap-
tismus non opponitur externo Ioannis baptismo. . . . Ioannes nihil
praeter fas sibi usurpat, quia autorem baptismi sui Christum habet, in quo constat signi veritas."*[12] To be sure he, the Baptist, has
only the *"externi signi administratio,"*[13] the *"nuda dispensatio."*[14]
Those who see him, or the work of the Christian ministry, might
well ask about the meaning and legitimacy of what takes place.
The only possible answer is to refer to him who stands among you.
"Vis et efficacia penes unum Christum tota est."[15] He with his
baptism of the Spirit (of which later in v. 33) is the Lord with
whom water baptism stands or falls. For this reason in v. 27 (confirming the negation of vv. 20f.) the Baptist cannot warn enough
against failing to see the absolutely dependent and relative character of his mission: *"ne qua in parte honor illi perperam delatus
Christi praestantiam obscuret."*[16] His relation to Christ is like that
of water to the Spirit in baptism. He is truly and literally unworthy
to untie Christ's shoelaces. This Gospel does not mention the baptism of Jesus by John. It does not do so even later where it refers
to the sign which occurred on this occasion according to the Synoptics.[17] That Jesus' baptism by John was an offense, that the Evangelist wanted to suppress all recollection of it, need not be assumed.

---

[11]Bauer, loc. cit.

[12]Calvin, op. cit., col. 23. [See Eng. tr. p. 30: "the spiritual Baptism of
Christ is not distinctly contrasted with the external Baptism of John. . . . John
claims nothing beyond what is right for him, for the author of his Baptism is
Christ, in whom consists the truth of the sign."]

[13]Loc. cit. [See Eng. tr. p. 30: "administration of the outward sign."]

[14]Calvin, op. cit., col. 24. [See Eng. tr. p. 30: "bare administration."]

[15]Calvin, op. cit., col. 23. [See Eng. tr. p. 30: "All the power and efficacy
is in the hands of Christ alone."]

[16]Calvin, op. cit., col. 24. [See Eng. tr. pp. 30-31: "lest any degree of honour
wrongly given to him should obscure the superiority of Christ."]

[17]Cf. Mark 1:10f. and par.

But that the fact does not interest him cannot be contested, just as
the story of the temptation plainly does not interest him, or at any
rate not so much that he is ready to take the detour which would
be needed to reach his goal if he were to introduce these facts.
History for history's sake interests the Fourth Evangelist as little
as the first three. That[18] the Baptist yields to Jesus and in this way
finds his positive place, the *emprosthen mou gegonen* of v. 15 and
v. 30, is thus more important for him than anything that might be
included in the *opisō mou erchomenos*. This is the relation of his
mission to the mission of Christ. *In* this relation it *stands*. It *has*
its legitimacy. There *is* a sacrament. This is what we must undoubtedly supply in the sense of the text.

We come to the conclusion in vv. 32-34. How does the Baptist
know what those who ask him (v. 26b) and all those to whom he
witnesses do not know? Again the *kagō ouk ēdein auton* in v. 33
emphasizes that he did not draw his knowledge of the Coming One
from himself, which might have given him some share in his dignity
at least in virtue of his special openness and receptivity, in virtue
of the knowledge that differentiates him from others. No, as concerns himself he stands in solidarity with those to whom v. 26b
refers. It is thus appropriate to take the *kagō* to mean "I also." He
knows what the others do not know because *tetheamai to*
pneuma . . . , v. 32. *"Impropria est vel figurata loquutio,"* Calvin
rightly comments on this *tetheamai*.[19] That the Baptist saw the
Spirit physically is not the meaning of the text. He perceived him
as the glory of the Logos is perceived in v. 14. What he saw physically — in this light we are also to construe the *idēs* of v. 33 — was
the sign introduced by the *hōs,* i.e., the dove. This sign need not
be dissolved into a *"figurata loquutio."* *Hōs peristeran* does not
mean that he saw something like a dove but that he physically saw
a real dove, and that on the basis of the sign offered by the dove
he perceived that the Spirit was present (namely, present in Jesus).
It is decisively important for a proper understanding that we let
this dove be a real dove — why not? — and that we understand the
whole statement in the light of the *hōs peristeran*. The *katabainein*

---

[18]A: "That the *Word* became flesh, that is more important for him than
that the Word became *flesh,* that."

[19]Calvin, op. cit., col. 27. [See Eng. tr. p. 34: "This is an unliteral and
figurative expression."]

and the *menein ep' auton* both apply to the dove. The question which W. Bauer thinks was probably a difficulty for the author, namely, whether the incarnate Logos had still to *receive* the Spirit, is thus a pointless one.[20] Naturally he did not, but nothing is said about any such receiving either here or in the Synoptic accounts of the baptism of Jesus. The *dove* is said to descend from heaven and to rest or alight or hover (as the star did over the house at Bethlehem [Matt. 2:9]) upon or over him, *ep' auton,* and not *en autǭ* as it would have to be if it were a matter of the Spirit himself, of the *menein* [*en*][21] which so often occurs in this Gospel, the abiding of the Father or of Christ in believers or of believers in him. The whole context shows that the stress is on this *ep' auton.* The sign is meant to be a sign. It is not a matter of someone receiving the Spirit. If we have the Spirit descending, then all kinds of material inconsistencies arise and the whole process and context become completely obscure. It is a matter of someone who already has the Spirit. On the basis of the visible physical sign which is given with the *katabainein* and *menein* of the dove, he who baptizes with water perceives who it is that baptizes with the Spirit. *Houtos estin ho baptizōn.* v. 33 says expressly in announcing the sign. It thus defines the *houtos estin* of v. 30 and confirms historically the *houtos ēn* of v. 2 and v. 15. According to v. 33 the Baptist did not recognize even the sign of the dove directly, or grasp its significance of himself. This is where the second *ouk ędein* comes in. He was first told by him who sent him that this sign would have this meaning, that it would denote the presence of the fulness of the Spirit in this man. He who is singled out by this sign is the one who baptizes with the Holy Spirit, i.e., the one who lends force and efficacy, or truth, to the administration and dispensation of water baptism, the author of baptism, the founder of the sacrament in its totality. Nothing at all is said about the baptism of the Spirit, which becomes an event in Christ, suppressing or replacing or supplanting water baptism, and this cannot be the meaning of the text, for from the very first the Christian church has adopted and continued the Baptist's *baptizein en hydati.*

V. 34 impressively sums up the whole content of vv. 29-33. This is — here for the first time we now find the leading concept

[20]W. Bauer, op. cit., p. 36.
[21]*en* is added from A.

which has long since been given its full content by the prologue —
the *Son* of God, unless, as Zahn prefers,[22] we are to read *huios
eklektos.* If, as Clemen declares, the descent of a bird can be proved
to be for ancient thinking a divine sign on the choice of a king,[23]
and if this is relevant in the present context, that reading, which
seems incontestably to be more original, would have some probability. However that may be, the perfect-present *heōraka kai memartyrēka* which sums up this result of the story of the Baptist
shows that the Baptist's seeing and work, and his baptism, continue even in the presence of him to whom he bears witness. Perhaps like the law in Rom. 3:31, they are not abolished but
established by faith. There *is* a sacrament; perhaps this is how we
might summarize the conclusion of this story of the witness of John.

---

[22]Zahn, op. cit., p. 126.

[23]C. Clemen, *Religionsgeschichtliche Erklärung des Neuen Testaments. Die
Abhängigkeit des ältesten Christentums von nichtjüdischen Religionen und phi-
losophischen Systemen.* 2nd ed. (Giessen, 1924), p. 124.

VERSES 35-51

Again the following day John stood there and two of his disciples, and when he looked at Jesus who was passing by, he says: There is the Lamb of God. And his disciples heard him say this and followed Jesus. But Jesus turned, saw that they followed him, and said to them: What do you seek? And they said to him: Rabbi (which means Teacher), where do you stay? He says to them: Come and you will see. Then they came and saw where he stayed, and they stayed with him that day. It was about the tenth hour. Andrew, the brother of Simon Peter, was one of the two who heard that from John and followed him. He first finds his brother Simon and says to him: We have found the Messiah (which means Christ). He led him to Jesus. When Jesus saw him, he said: You are Simon, the son of John, you shall be called Cephas (which means Peter). The next day he wanted to go to Galilee and find Philip. And Jesus says to him: Follow me. Now Philip was from Bethsaida, the city of Andrew and Peter. Philip finds Nathanael and says to him: We have found him of whom Moses in the law and the prophets wrote: Jesus, the son of Joseph of Nazareth. And Nathanael said to him: Can any good thing come out of Nazareth? Philip says to him: Come and see. Jesus saw Nathanael coming to him and said of him: This is a true Israelite in whom is no falsity. Nathanael says to him: How do you know me? Jesus answered and said to him: Before Philip called you, I saw you under the fig tree. Nathanael answered him: Rabbi, you are the Son of God, you are the king of Israel. Jesus answered and said to him: Because I told you I saw you under the fig tree, do you believe? You shall see greater things than these. And he said to him: Truly, truly, I tell you, you shall see heaven opened, and the angels of God ascending and descending on the Son of Man.

This section deals with the disciples of Jesus in the strictest sense, with the apostles and how there came to be such. Let us first touch on certain more external problems. Reference is made specifically to five disciples. The names of four are given, Andrew and his brother Simon, Philip, and Nathanael. The name of the fifth, or rather of the first or second, is not given. If we stress the *ton idion* in v. 41, and perhaps read *prōtos* with Zahn[1] ("first *his* brother"), then the "first" is saying that Andrew was the first to find his brother and tell him about the Messiah. We may tacitly assume, then, that the other disciple mentioned in vv. 35-40, who is not named, also found his brother. If we compare the list of apostles in the Synoptics,[2] we find that the constant sequence is: Peter and Andrew, John and James, Philip and Bartholomew, etc. The presentation here agrees in putting Peter and Andrew first and it also puts Philip early, so that if we have a reference to a second pair of brothers in v. 41, it seems likely that the *idios adelphos* of the unnamed disciple of v. 40 is in fact James, and that this disciple himself, whom vv. 35-40 have in mind, is John, the son of Zebedee. And in this case the hypothesis is unavoidable that there is an intimate relation between the author of the Gospel and this disciple who is introduced so mysteriously and almost as a mere shadow. But another conjecture arises out of this glance at the Synoptic list of the apostles. First surfacing in the Middle Ages, this conjecture is that Nathanael is perhaps the same as the Bartholomew, son of Tholmai, who is mentioned there in sixth place.[3] Or may it be that Nathanael, who according to 21:2 belongs to Cana in Galilee, is not one of the twelve? Augustine thought not.[4] Or is he perhaps identical with the Matthias of Acts? Or is Nathanael — as Hausrath, Schmiedel,[5] and others conjecture — a code name for Paul? Or is he not a concrete historical figure at all but (Bauer) a "type for those who do indeed doubt but without closing

---

[1] T. Zahn, op. cit., p. 134.
[2] Cf. Mark 3:16-19 and par.
[3] Cf. W. Bauer. op. cit., p. 40.
[4] Augustine, op. cit.. VII. 17 (pp. 126f.). [See Eng. tr. p. 34.]
[5] On Hausrath and Schmiedel cf. H. J. Holtzmann. op. cit.. p. 70.

themselves off against better insights"?[6] In such questions one can
conjecture many things in John but affirm or deny little with certainty. That the calling of the disciples in John does not put the
disciples at work in Galilee but in the middle of the Baptist movement in Perea can be explained, if one has a taste for harmonizing
and finds pleasure in it as Augustine did,[7] by supposing that the
decisive or externally definitive call to true *akolouthein* is the second one that is recounted by the Synoptists. One cannot deny, of
course, that John puts the true calling here, i.e., the calling that is
for him essential and decisive in principle as far as their relationship is concerned. He brings it into connection with the Baptist, so
that his portrayal is distinctive vis-à-vis the Synoptists. But let us
turn now to the matter itself. Five points seem to me to be decisive
for our understanding of the text.

1. The Baptist is the primary agent in the whole process that
is described (vv. 35-37). He sets the ball rolling. His disciples (v. 35)
are the first two who become disciples of Jesus and by whom the
discovery of the Messiah is propagated. It is his pointing finger, his
saying "There is the Lamb of God," that they follow when they
become disciples of Jesus. Note the repetition *dyo tōn akousantōn
para Iōannou* (v. 40) and consider *which* disciple is one of the two.
The work of John, his witness as it is depicted in the prologue in
vv. 19-34, now bears fruit. *His* disciples become Jesus' disciples.
This connection — we must say this in augmentation of what we
have said about the absence of any account of the baptism — is very
strongly underlined by the Evangelist when he depicts the calling
of the disciples, and truly not to the disadvantage of the Baptist.

2. Over the decisive moment in the whole process, namely,
the occurrence of the encounters that underlie the disciple relationship, there lies a noteworthy veil of contingency, unimportance, and
lack of emphasis. Note the verb *heuriskein*, which occurs five times
with a certain monotony. Thus Jesus himself finds Philip (v. 43);
Andrew finds his brother Simon (v. 41); Philip finds Nathanael
(v. 45); and Andrew and the unknown disciple (v. 41), and also
Philip (v. 45), find the Messiah. Everywhere there is finding. As
though drawn by invisible threads the persons concerned come
together. At the right moment — how is unimportant — they are at

---

[6]Bauer, op. cit., p. 41.
[7]Augustine, op. cit., VII, 9 (p. 119). [See Eng. tr. p. 51.]

the right place for one another. This is the impression left by the
verses. Related to this, interesting in its very lack of interest, is the
little conversation in vv. 38-39. What do you seek? This is the first
saying of Jesus himself in the Gospel. One might seriously think
that in this question the Evangelist was thinking of profound and
ultimate things full of weighty content. But he does nothing to
indicate what they might be. The counterquestion: *Rhabbi, pou
meneis?* certainly means: Where do you stay? Where is the tent or
house in which you live? And when Jesus replies, Come and see,
we certainly might look ahead from this *opsesthe* to that of v. 51,
but in the first instance v. 39b confirms in very banal fashion that
they really came and saw *pou menei,* where he lived. And then?
we might ask with bated breath. Then they spent the day with him.
Certainly there is some emphasis, but it is the toneless one of a
note of the time: about the tenth hour, or four in the afternoon.
What is the point of this *hōra hōs dekatē*? Certainly it is not a
reference to [the][8] lapsing of the time of the Ten Commandments,
as Augustine thought.[9] It simply tells us that it happened then. But
what happened then? The record does not tell us. The Evangelist
did not think it necessary to tell us about the "hour-long conversation" which took place according to Zahn,[10] or the "insight into
the goal of Jesus" which Schlatter derived[11] from it.[12] This is an
encounter whose How he obviously wanted to keep out of the grasp
of all earth-bound pragmatism. Jesus and his disciples, and later
the disciples and disciples, find one another for various good reasons. The Why and How are quite unimportant. The important
thing is simply that they do so. When John's witness has set the
ball rolling, this finding just takes place. Later, by hindsight, one
might realize that the *erchesthe kai opsesthe* (v. 39) and the *erchou
kai ide* (v. 46) say more than appears on the surface. But precisely
then one will not destroy the unassuming veil that lies over these
scenes, e.g., by discovering with Zahn in v. 38 that Jesus hears the
steps of those who follow him, and for this reason turns around
and addresses them, or by finding in the *pou meneis* (v. 39) the

---

[8]A adds the "the."

[9]Augustine, loc. cit. [See Eng. tr. p. 51.]

[10]Zahn, op. cit., p. 131.

[11]A and B both have "found" for "derived."

[12]Schlatter, op. cit., p. 16.

desire of the two to speak with him undisturbed.[13] How can anyone be so ponderous?

3. On the side of Jesus a distinctive feature of the relationship that rests on these mysterious encounters is that from the very first glance he is not getting to know these people but he already knows them. Naturally this is a miraculous or *divine* knowledge. The *sy klēthēsę̄ Kēphas* is prophecy and not just characterization (v. 42), and v. 48 shows that there is no pragmatically intelligible source (*pothen*) for the knowledge of Nathanael. But we should not exaggerate. John's Gospel is not an unbroken chain of such miracles. Things have been pushed too far in this direction in relation to this section, and it has been robbed of much of its content as a result. The depicted divine knowledge of Jesus is not at all a knowledge of everything possible. The final point of the section is not to plunge us into astonishment at such omniscience. Let us cling to the fact that the theme is the rise of the band of disciples. The miraculous knowledge of Jesus here concerns not only who the disciples are at this moment but who they will become in the future in his service (v. 42) and who they have been before (v. 48). The impression grows that they come because they have no option but to come, because they are predestined, or, perhaps more exactly, foreseen, and then called and brought to an awareness of their own true existence by Jesus, who has long since known them better than they know themselves. Once in v. 43 there sounds forth the distinctively Synoptic "Follow me," and following (*akolouthein*) also plays a great role in vv. 37, 38, 40. But not an *important* role, one must say. "In his mercy he has seen you before you knew him, when you lay under sin. Have we first visited Christ, and not he us? Have we, the sick, come to the physician, and not the physician to the sick?" This is how Augustine,[14] surely catching the sense of the text, preached on the verse about Nathanael. We would do well to insist on this fact that Jesus comes first, on his primacy in principle in establishing the relationship with the disciples. This is the issue in the knowledge of Jesus that is depicted here. It is the same primacy as is later reflected in the saying in 15:16: "You have not chosen me, but I have chosen you." If this is correct, then we have good reason to suspect the inference that the *sy ei Simōn*, etc.

---

[13]Zahn, op. cit., pp. 129f.

[14]Augustine, op. cit., VII, 21 (p. 131). [See Eng. tr. pp. 55f.]

(v. 42), is a miracle of omniscience in virtue of which Jesus knew this first name and the family name.[15] What would be the point of such knowledge? It is evident from the parallel in Matt. 16:18 that in the first clause Jesus is saying something that is well-known — that Andrew told him[16] is naturally a quite unnecessary and tasteless assertion. All that Jesus is saying is that this is now your name. But in the second clause (although with no adversative particle) Jesus says something which is not known. Here is the prophecy: "You shall be called Cephas." This man is given a name and a position before he has ever spoken a word, let alone shown himself worthy. He is greeted with this institution to an office for which he seems to have none of the prerequisites. In the mind of John this is the real miracle in Jesus' knowledge of Simon and his saying about him. And it is miraculous enough, although it is not a marvel, but meaningful and illuminating regarding the way in which the disciples are to be understood. A miracle of omniscience relative to the man's civil name would simply be disruptive in this connection.

Let us look more closely at the verses about Nathanael (vv. 45ff.) in which this element, the thought of election, is especially prominent. What is important here, and what is not important? It is certainly not important that Nathanael first resists and then comes. Note in this regard how incidental the *erchomenon pros auton* (v. 47) is. Again, the whole process of fetching by Philip (vv. 45-46) is unimportant. Why it is depicted so expressly is shown by the *pro tou se Philippon phōnēsai* in v. 48. What is important — v. 50 comes back to it — is the *eiden,* along with the saying in which Jesus sums it up in v. 47, and later the second and explanatory *eidon* of vv. 48 and 50. Jesus knows Nathanael. He knows what he has been, just as he knows what Simon finally will be, so finally that with a view to it he gives to him, as to a baptismal candidate, his new and proper name. Jesus knows Nathanael — in my view everything crystallizes around this saying — as a true Israelite, as one who is a real member of God's chosen people. The term "Israelite" has here this theocratic and predestinarian significance. In no circumstances could *Ioudaios* be used here, and this not because Nathanael is from Cana in Galilee. He belongs to Israel. The derogatory answer which Nathanael gives in v. 46 to the joyful mes-

---

[15]Holtzmann, op. cit., p. 67; Zahn, op. cit., p. 136; Bauer, op. cit., pp. 37f.
[16]So B. Weiss according to Holtzmann, op. cit., p. 67.

sage of Philip tends to present this fact as a hidden one. But it is
not hidden from the eyes of Jesus. Note the transition from v. 46
to v. 47. "Come and see" is Philip's answer to Nathanael's rebuff.
But the continuation does not say that Nathanael came and saw.
It says the very opposite, namely, that Jesus saw Nathanael. Nathanael is seen; this is the point. Jesus sees him before he sees
Jesus, before he has even heard of him (v. 48). What vv. 45-46
recounted was simply an interlude that is now left behind. "I saw
you under the fig tree" — before Philip called you.

What is the point of the fig tree? The usual interpretation of
the saying is this. Under this fig tree, as is common under trees,
Nathanael was reflecting upon something decisively important, upon
something to do with his inner life, perhaps his position vis-à-vis
the hope of Israel. It was in this situation that Jesus saw him from
afar in that miraculous way. That we are told nothing about this
situation apart from the three words *hypo tēn sykēn* is for all lovers
of conversion stories an unfortunate circumstance if this interpretation is correct. To me it seems to be so sentimental as to be quite
incredible. And since it rests on pure association one might ask
whether other associations might not be equally valid. Augustine[17]
sought to understand[18] by the fig tree the shadow of death. He
appealed in support to the familiar fig leaves of Gen. 3:7. This view
has at least much more substance than that Christian[19] garden
romanticism. Closer to the text and context, it seems to me, is the
reminder that in 1 Kings 5:5; Mic. 4:4; Zech. 3:10 sitting or dwelling under the vine and fig tree characterizes the secure life of Israel
in the age of messianic peace. Why should not this understanding
be regulative here where Nathanael is called a true Israelite? This
eliminates a second miracle, the second miracle of remote vision,
which in the light of day proves to be superfluous and confusing,
although it is not my purpose to eliminate as many miracles as
possible from the text, only miracles that are imagined to be contained in the text. On this view, we do not have a second miraculous
insight. With the stress on *pro tou phōnēsai,* we have a second
statement, this time in Old Testament terms, of the insight of v. 47,
namely, that Nathanael is one of God's elect. The saying does not

---

[17]Augustine, op. cit., VII, 21 (pp. 130f.). [See Eng. tr. p. 55.]
[18]A and B have "see" for "understand."
[19]A has "pietistic."

refer to some garden experience of Nathanael under a real fig tree, but as a *figurata loquutio,* perhaps based on v. 47, it refers to the foreordained nature of this man, which has its original necessity from God, and the eschatological fulfilment of which is now anticipated. Before you saw and heard me, I saw you sheltered, saved, secure, and blessed under the fig tree, i.e., in the midst of the messianic kingdom. With this the reply of Nathanael, especially in the second half: "You are the King of Israel" (v. 49b), fits in very well as the thankful homage of the one who is thus addressed. Other explanations can do no real justice to this saying. They find no necessity for it, at any rate in the context.

4. What characterizes the position of the disciples in this relationship is the full confession of the Messiah which sounds forth on their lips, and does so before Jesus has said or done anything, before they themselves have taken even any preparatory steps behind him. When Jesus tells Nathanael that he knew him, and before Nathanael knew Jesus, there follows the recognition and confession of the one addressed: Rabbi, you are the Son of God (v. 49). This is also the logic behind v. 41 and v. 45. The directness with which the disciples are at once at the goal even at the very beginning of the way was too much even for Calvin, and so, obviously trying to slow down the process, he thought he could ascribe to Philip in the saying of v. 45 two crass errors, first, that he regarded Jesus as the son of Joseph, and second, that he thought Nazareth was his home town.[20] But there is no substance in this, nor in the view of modern exegetes that the *huios tou Iōsēph* proves that John's Gospel neither knows nor wants to know anything of the virgin birth.[21] That saying of Philip has obvious significance in relation to his conversation with Nathanael. Philip is just as much at the goal of knowledge as Andrew before him and Nathanael after him. As the Evangelist portrays it, knowing Christ is a decision which is either taken or not taken, but which, when it is taken, is taken with all its implications. One might call this portrait unpsychological. It is indeed, and this is the good thing about it. A development, a gradual emergence of this knowledge is not to be seen in fact in the Synoptics either. If confession of the Messiah

---

[20]Calvin, op. cit., col. 33. [See Eng. tr. pp. 40f.]
[21]Cf. Holtzmann, op. cit., pp. 67f.

comes there at a lofty turning point[22] in Matt. 16, then in express contradiction of all psychology and pedagogics, Matt. 16:17 says: "Flesh and blood have not revealed this to you, but my Father in heaven." Recognition of the Messiah comes directly from above or not at all. It is also to the point to say expressly (as the passage does) that historically considered it is both the beginning and the goal.[23]

5. The section shows that entry into the relationship of a disciple is not only the result but also the beginning of seeing what is to be seen in Jesus. This is how one must expound the "Come and see" (v. 39; cf. v. 46). One comes as one self-evidently must because one *is* seen (v. 47) and then on this basis one sees. *What* does one see? I have suggested already that the *menein* of vv. 38-39 is freighted with a sense which goes beyond the concrete one of having one's dwelling. But here perhaps we are to think only of the fact that there is another abiding of Christ and his people beyond that concrete and practical one. In the light of v. 51, where *opsesthe* recurs, we are perhaps to think back to that *menein*. Yet an allegorical interpretation of vv. 50-51 does not commend itself; as and because Nathanael sees that he is known by Jesus — "because I said to you that I saw you under the fig tree" — he believes, *pisteueis*. But *meizō toutōn opsē*. The wonderful knowledge and the faith that rests upon it, the messianic knowledge and the messianic confession, are as such only a beginning. "You shall see" (v. 51; cf. v. 29) — what? Answer (introduced by the solemn Johannine "Truly, truly"): "That which Jacob saw." For undoubtedly there is here another reference back to the Old Testament, this time to Gen. 28:10ff. But what is the issue in this reminiscence? The opening of heaven, the descent of the angels, the dealings that are thus initiated between earth and heaven? Perhaps with some stress, as in Zahn,[24] on the fact that *apsabainein* comes first, with the implication that these dealings have already begun? Yet what Jacob saw in Gen. 28 when he woke up from sleep is remarkably not at all the truth that there is such an opening of heaven and that there are these dealings between heaven and earth. The focal point of his reflections is that these things are *here* in the place where he un-

---

[22]A: "at a high point and turning point" (B is perhaps a slip in dictation).
[23]A: "it is not the beginning but the goal."
[24]Zahn, op. cit., p. 145.

suspectingly laid himself down: "Surely the Lord is in this place, and I did not know it," and he was afraid and said: "How holy is this place. This is none other than the house of God and the gate of heaven." He thus calls the place Beth-El. If this Old Testament commentary is to be regarded as authentic, then in v. 51 the accent falls on the *epi ton huion tou anthrōpou* (as it does on the *ep' auton* in v. 32). That here, in and through the known Messiah (i.e., the Son of Man), the gate of heaven is now seen to be open;[25] that being known, knowing, and confessing are only the introduction — to what? to a here and now of revelation, to a *holy* place, to *the* holy place on earth; that Jesus as the Messiah is Beth-El, where God is continually praised[26] — these are the "greater things" that they shall come to see (v. 50). This entry into Beth-El will then be, if one looks back from here, the secret of the *menein* of vv. 38-39.

---

[25]An allusion to the hymn "Jauchzet, ihr Himmel" (1731) by G. Tersteegen, verse 4: "Here the gate of life is seen to be open."

[26]An allusion to the hymn "O Jerusalem, du schöne" by F. K. Hiller (1662-1726), verse 1 ("where God is continually revered").

INDEXES

I. SCRIPTURE REFERENCES

II. NAMES

III. SUBJECTS

IV. SELECT GREEK WORDS

ginōskein 71. 77f.
doxa 97ff.
exousia 73f.
erchesthai 51, 62, 68, 87
erchesthai opisō 105f.
zōē 38ff.
theasthai 96
idia/idioi 66f., 71f.
kai 84f., 116
kosmos 63f.
lambanein 70f., 78, 114f., 121
logos 22ff.
martyrein/martyria 16, 51, 59, 104f.,
  110, 134

menein 142, 148, 153
monogenēs 99f., 129
nomos 123
onoma 76
horan 126
pisteuein 71f., 75ff.
plērōma 115
sarx 87ff.
skēnoun 93ff.
skotia 45ff.
phōs 36f., 40, 60ff.
charis 100ff., 116ff.

LIBRARY, UNIVERSITY OF CHESTER